BISON
BOOKS

Chasing Geronimo

THE JOURNAL
OF LEONARD WOOD,
MAY-SEPTEMBER 1886

Edited and with an introduction and epilogue by
JACK C. LANE

With a new preface by the editor

UNIVERSITY OF NEBRASKA PRESS
LINCOLN AND LONDON

Library of Congress Cataloging-in-Publication Data
Wood, Leonard, 1860–1927.
Chasing Geronimo: the journal of Leonard Wood, May-September
1886 / Leonard Wood; edited and with an introduction and epilogue by
Jack C. Lane; with a new preface by the editor.
p. cm.
Originally published: Albuquerque: University of New Mexico Press,
1970.
Includes bibliographical references and index.
ISBN 978-0-8032-2527-5 (paper: alk. paper)
1. Geronimo, 1829–1909. 2. Apache Indians—Wars, 1883–1886.
3. Apache Indians—Biography. 4. Wood, Leonard, 1860–1927—
Diaries. 5. Soldiers—United States—Diaries. I. Lane, Jack C., 1932–
II. Title.
E83.88.w6 2009
970.004'97—dc22
2009031138

Preface to the Bison Books Edition

Since the publication of Leonard Wood's journal thirty-eight years ago, interest in Geronimo and the campaign to capture him has not lagged. Two early biographies of Geronimo, both sympathetic to the Apache warrior's struggle—Alexander B. Adams, *Geronimo: A Biography* (1971) and Angie Debo, *Geronimo: The Man, His Time, His Place* (1976)—appeared shortly after my own publication, along with reprints of John Bourke's *On the Border with Crook* (1971) and George Crook's *Resume of Operations Against the Apache Indians*. More recently, other important studies have been published: C. L. Sonnichsen, ed., *Geronimo and the End of the Apache Wars* (1986), reprinted in 1990, followed by David Roberts, *Once They Moved Like the Wind: Cochise, Geronimo, and the Apache Wars* (1993). In 2000 Louis Kraft detailed Charles Gatewood's role in the Apache Wars in *Gatewood and Geronimo*, and he recently edited Gatewood's own account of his experiences in *Lt. Charles Gatewood and His Apache War Memoirs* (2005). It now seems the appropriate time to once again make available a primary source that provides important information about and insight into the last Apache military campaign. The present reprint of *Chasing Geronimo*, with the introduction, epilogue, and notes, remains the same as the original publication. Although with hindsight I would change some of the descriptive language in the introduction and epilogue, on the whole I think both have stood the test of time.

Jack C. Lane, Emeritus
Rollins College

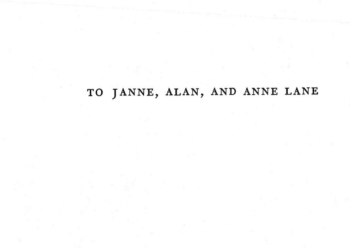

TO JANNE, ALAN, AND ANNE LANE

Preface

Leonard Wood seriously began keeping a record of his observations and impressions during his trip West in 1885. He continued the practice throughout his lifetime. The result is a voluminous record; and because Wood held several high military and public posts, it is an important primary source. But the diary is uneven in quality. It has large gaps when he recorded nothing, and much of it contains trivia significant only to the biographer. Still there are enough significant entries in the later diary to make it a prime source of information for students of American military, political, and diplomatic history in the first three decades of the twentieth century.

The journal kept by Wood during the Geronimo campaign differs from his later record in two ways. First, he kept a more detailed account of the campaign than of any of his later activities. He clearly sensed the significance of the event and wanted to record it; in addition, journal-keeping was still a novelty to him. He therefore assiduously recorded his observations at every spare moment.

Second, the journal of the Geronimo campaign is much more impersonal than his later writing. It is not totally devoid of impressionistic writing; one of its conspicuous characteristics is its "human" touch—its details of foods, wounds, quarrels, dress, hardships, and so on. But on the whole, Wood seems more interested in recording what he observed and what happened to the expedition than in expressing his personal views. Robert A. Brown—besides Wood and Henry Lawton the most active participant in the campaign—later concluded that the journal was "remarkably accurate" but that its greater value lay "in the fact that the narrative is confined almost entirely to matters that come under [Wood's] own immediate observation and knowledge." (Brown to Hagedorn, 1929, Papers of Hermann Hagedorn, Library of Congress, Washington, D.C.)

Wood's usual method of record-keeping was to jot down brief notes on a pad and later to amplify them in narrative form, a practice he followed in composing the journal of the Geronimo campaign. His original notes, however, were amazingly complete; moreover, the notes and the amplification agree entirely.

The journal, with notes and narrative, is part of the Papers of Leonard Wood (Library of Congress, Washington, D.C.). Also included in the papers is an eleven-page summary of the campaign, written by Wood at the request of Nelson A. Miles. This summary was later published in Miles's *Personal Recollections and Observations of General Nelson A. Miles* (Chicago: The Werner Company, 1896).

I wish to express my appreciation to Allan Millett for reading the manuscript and for offering valuable suggestions, to the New Mexico University Press for its help and cooperation, to Rollins College for financial aid, and to my wife Janne for her assistance in correcting and improving my writing.   J.C.L.

Rollins College
Winter Park, Florida

Contents

Preface to the Bison Books Edition   v

Preface   ix

Introduction   3

PART I: ORGANIZING THE EXPEDITION   23

Chapter 1: "The Right Sort of White Men"   25

PART II: THE CHASE   47

Chapter 2: Searching for Trails in Sonora Province   49

Chapter 3: A Coming Fight   59

Chapter 4: The Depths of Despair   73

PART III: THE SURRENDER   85

Chapter 5: A New Policy   87

Chapter 6: The Problems of Negotiation and Surrender   103

Epilogue   113

Notes   119

Selected Bibliography   141

Index   147

Illustrations

Following page 84

Leonard Wood in Arizona, 1886
Fort Huachuca, Arizona Territory
Lawton's column on the trail, by Remington
Search party seeking lost livestock
Apache captives at a rest stop, 1886
Pack mule loaded with mess boxes
Packer hitching a cinch, by Remington
Diagram for tieing a diamond hitch
Geronimo in 1886

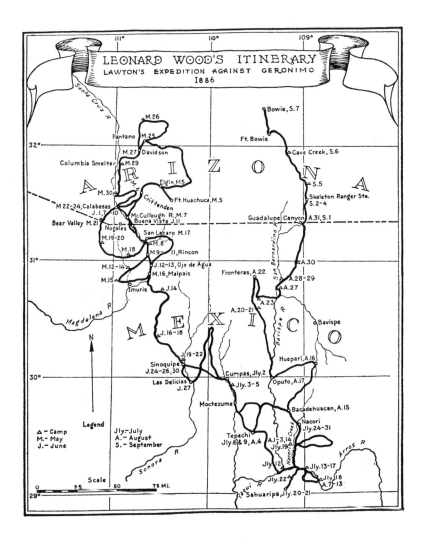

LEONARD WOOD'S ITINERARY
LAWTON'S EXPEDITION AGAINST GERONIMO
1886

Chasing Geronimo

Introduction

I

Those who are familiar with American history in the first two decades of the twentieth century know that Leonard Wood was a prominent public figure. He was active in the preparedness movement before America's intervention in the First World War, and he became the leading candidate for the Republican presidential nomination in 1920.

Those familiar with military history of the same period also know that Wood was an outstanding officer in the American Army. By 1917, he had become the Army's ranking regular officer. Behind him lay an outstanding military career which included such offices as military governor of Cuba and the Moro Province in the Philippines, commander of the Philippine Division, and chief of staff of the Army. His promotions in rank were similarly astounding. Before the outbreak of the Spanish-American War, Wood was a captain in the Medical Corps. He was appointed colonel at the outset of the war and achieved considerable fame in Cuba as the commander of the popular Rough Riders. Shortly after the war, he rose to major general of the Volunteer Army. While military governor of Cuba, Wood was appointed brigadier general in the Regular Army by President McKinley. Two years later President Roosevelt appointed him major general; in 1910, less than ten years after he had become a regular officer, Wood was named Chief of Staff, the highest office in the Army.

Although his military career as a regular line officer began in 1901, Wood's military life began in 1886 when he accepted a commission as assistant surgeon in the Army Medical Corps. Before this appointment, Wood had spent a childhood in New England, four years at Harvard Medical School, and one year at an unsuccessful private medical practice in Boston. In May 1885, after passing the Army Medical Corps examination, he accepted a commission in the Medical Corps. Because there were no positions vacant at the time, he agreed to serve as contract surgeon until a vacancy occurred.

Ordered to report to the commanding officer of the Department of Arizona, on July 4, 1885, he arrived at Fort Huachuca, Arizona Territory, where he was attached as medical officer to Troop B, 4th Cavalry, commanded by Captain Henry Lawton. For such an ambitious and adventurous young man, the assignment could not have been more propitious. Within a year after his arrival, Lawton's troop was chosen to conduct a campaign against the Apache Indians led by the notorious Geronimo—a campaign that would end in the final capture of the wily Indian and his band and bring fame and advancement to both Lawton and Wood.

II

Indian fighting became the American Army's principal occupation after 1865. Such activity was not new to the Army; it had been involved in Indian pacification since the turn of the century. It was a singularly thankless task. While reformers in the East decried the harsh treatment of the Indians by the government, and particularly the Army's pursuit of them, local residents inundated Washington with complaints of the Army's inability to prevent widespread depredations. Moreover, since the Interior Department managed the Indians, the Army was called in only

4

in times of crises when the tribes had already gone on the war path. While this was perhaps theoretically the proper use of the Army, many civilian agents were either inexperienced, incompetent, or involved in the notorious "Indian Ring" that systematically exploited the Indians after 1865 and frequently drove them off the reservations. The Indians tended to trust some of the Army officers whom they had fought and negotiated and to distrust most of the agents who administered to their needs when they returned to the reservations. Time and time again the Army officers were forced to remain idle while agreements, which they had so painstakingly negotiated with the Indians, were broken by the Bureau of Indian Affairs.[1]

The post-Civil War Indian fighting army became a rugged, disciplined, professional force. From 1877 to 1898 it fluctuated in size between 24,000 and 27,000 and was scattered among 255 military posts. Because the guerrilla-type warfare of the Indians demanded mobility for their pursuers, the Regular Army rarely mobilized more than a few hundred men for a campaign. In the early years after the Civil War the officers, trained and experienced in conventional warfare, found it difficult to adjust to the hit-and-run tactics of the Indians. Given limited resources and manpower, they found the Indian a rugged adversary. In fact, as one authority has suggested, a better organized, better disciplined adversary using the Indian's guerrilla tactics might have fought the existing Regular Army to a standoff. The fact that the Regular Army possessed the particular attributes the Indian tribes lacked —that is, organization and discipline—explains much of its ultimate success in pacification. Specifically, superior organization allowed the Army to fight in the winter, when the Indian was forced into camps to avoid exposure. The freezing winters gave the Army, provided with warm clothing and constant supplies, an opportunity to strike the Indian when the latter's most important tactic—mobility—was weakest. "General Winter," more often than a superior fighting force, gave the Army some of its most decisive victories against the Indian.[2]

The Apaches, located in the administrative area of the Department of Arizona, perfected hit-and-run guerrilla warfare. The Apache tribes never combined, as the Plains Indians occasionally did, into a massive force. Instead, they operated in small raiding parties rarely numbering over one hundred. Intermittently, a branch of the tribe would illegally leave the reservation and embark on a campaign of plunder and destruction that would leave countless homes burned and scores of dead in its wake. Long years of hatred and struggle against the civil authorities had turned the Apache into a revengeful hostile. Even those who were highly critical of the government's Indian policy and sympathetic with the plight of the Indian agreed that the Apaches "were the most savage and intractable Indians in the country."[3]

But it was not savagery alone that made the Apache the Army's most impervious foe in the 1870s and 1880s; it was also his seemingly unlimited ability to endure with only the bare necessities for long periods of time in the almost impenetrable barren mountains and deserts of southern Arizona and northern Mexico. This scorching, arid land, so forbidding to the white man, was a natural habitat for several Apache tribes. In fact, many of their grievances arose when the government moved them from their native mountains to the Arizona lowlands. Organizing themselves into small bands, they ravaged the Arizona territory at will until, pursued too closely by the Army, they retired into the almost impregnable strongholds in the Sierra Madre Mountains.

In 1871, the Army assigned as commander of the Department of Arizona the only officer who succeeded in pacifying the Apaches before their displacement in 1886. General George Crook was perhaps the Army's most skillful and capable Indian fighter. Veteran of the Civil War and several Indian campaigns, he was idolized by those who served under him and respected by those whom he fought. Crook was one of the few Americans that the wild and unapproachable Apache ever really trusted. He gained their trust with a program combining dogged pursuit and judicious treatment. The bewhiskered veteran was, as one of his supporters observed, "one of the most absolutely just and true friends the Indian had ever known."[4] He fought the Apache with vigor; but he used military force merely to reinforce his diplomatic strategy, which included conciliation, education, and playing off one tribe against another. Diplomacy and force, however, were only means to an end. His aim was to bring the Indians into conference and convince them that their survival lay only in returning to the reservations. He patiently listened to their grievances and consistently promised fairer treatment if they would return.

Once he had them on the reservation, Crook made it possible for the Indians to attain some self-sufficiency by raising their own food; he gave them an opportunity for self-government through the use of their own police. In short, he provided them with a sense of self-respect. In addition, with authority from the government, Crook made the Apaches accountable to his officers rather than to the Indian agent, although the latter was expected to work cooperatively with the military agents. This increase in the authority of Army officers over the Indians was designed to overcome what Crook considered the major problem in dealing with the Indians: unjust and unfair treatment by civilian agents.[5]

Another Crook policy was that of using Indians to fight Indians. He was absolutely certain that without the aid of Indian scouts, white soldiers were incapable of capturing the Apache if he chose to remain in the wilds of northern Mexico. While the Apache seemed to thrive on arid land and in the hot climate, the regular soldier was forced to burden himself with long supply trains. Crook came to believe that in a kind of fighting which put a premium on mobility and endurance, neither the regular infantry nor the regular cavalry could cope with the Apache. Britton Davis, one of Crook's trusted aides, believed that regular troops were a positive hinderance. Thus, while Crook still relied on regular troops and pack trains, the key to his system was the use of well-trained Indian scouts commanded by a regular officer.[6]

Within three years after Crook was assigned to the Department of Arizona, he had pacified the Apaches, and while he remained there the Indians resided peacefully on the reservations. But when Indian problems in Montana caused the War Department to transfer Crook to the Department of the Platte, the relaxation of his firm hand seems to have precipitated a massive Apache defection from the reservations. Crook was returned in 1882 and began the process of pacification all over again. Primarily by using a large contingent of Apache Scouts—193 trained and commanded by Captain Emmet Crawford—and by taking advantage of an agreement between the United States and Mexico permitting regular troops to cross the border in pursuit of hostiles, Crook subdued the Apaches eight months after he resumed command. Under the control of regular officers they were settled on the San Carlos reservation. There they remained peacefully for two years, when, for reasons not quite clear, a group of malcontents led by the incorrigible Geronimo left the reservation on May 17, 1886, to begin the final and in some ways the most spectacular Indian campaign in the history of Indian fighting in the Southwest. For ten months the band moved in and out of their mountain fastnesses, raiding and looting, and burning homes and towns on both sides of the border. Before the campaign was over, one of Crook's most trusted aides, Captain Crawford, had been killed, the commander's policy of judicious negotiation and his Apache scout system had been discredited, and Crook had been replaced by an equally prominent Indian fighter, General Nelson A. Miles.[7]

Miles—the "brave peacock," as Theodore Roosevelt was later to call him—was an exceedingly ambitious officer on the way up at this point in his career. Without a formal military education (he had not attended West Point) Miles entered the Army at the outbreak of the Civil War as first lieutenant in the 22nd Massachusetts Volunteers. He advanced rapidly and by the end of the war was made brevet major general. After the war Miles accepted a commission as colonel in the Regular Army. A series of Indian campaigns, one of which culminated in the spectacular capture of the Nez Percé, had brought Miles honors and a promotion to brigadier. Contrary to the shy, modest, unassuming Crook, Miles was vain, pompous, and given to grandstanding. His spectacular rise from lieutenant in 1860 to general twenty years later had given him a self-opinionated, arrogant attitude which did not make him many friends. His marriage to the niece of Senator John Sherman and General William Sherman led many regular West Point graduates to see Miles' advancement more in terms of preference.[8] From a professional as well as a policy view, Miles was a natural enemy of General Crook and his followers.

In 1886, Miles was enjoying the pleasant life of commander of the Department of Missouri when the War Department ordered him to Arizona. He was anything but pleased with the assignment.[9] Not only did he dislike the Southwest, but the job did not offer prospects for his consuming ambition. The assignment could very easily damage his career as it had George Crook's. Aware that the commanding general of the Army, Philip Sheridan, was watching the campaign closely and knowing that Crook and his men were confident he could not succeed where they had failed, Miles reluctantly became Commander of the Department of Arizona in May 1886.[10]

Miles brought with him no new strategy for the capture of Geronimo. He did make clear, however, that he intended to operate on the theory that the Apaches must be taken by force and by force alone, an obvious thrust at Crook's diplomatic methods. Sheridan, who had lost confidence in Crook's extensive use of friendly Apache scouts,[11] advised Miles to make more effective use of regular troops in his campaign.[12] Crook and most of his officers did not believe white troops could compete with the Apache in his own country. The wildly rugged terrain, the blistering heat, and the aridity of the land gave the Apache, who was acclimated to these conditions, a distinct advantage. The American soldier, it was believed, did not possess the physical endurance nor did the Army possess the resources to capture the Apaches if the Indians wished to remain in the wilderness of the Sierra

Madre.[13] Miles knew all these arguments; but, if he wanted to please Sheridan and at the same time develop a different policy, he had no choice but to send regular troops into the wilds to run down the Apaches.

Like Crook, Miles retained the conventional strategy of converging columns; but he also tried to improve communications between the lightly equipped pursuing units and to select a group of men, carefully chosen for their tenacious will and physical endurance, to form the principal striking force. While other detachments stationed along the frontier gathered information on the movement of the Indians, the principal column was given the task of pursuing Geronimo until he and his band were captured or destroyed.[14]

This strategy differed from Crook's only in Miles' attitude toward the hostiles. It was a critical difference. Crook's policy had been to catch up with the Indians and enter into negotiations, where he would use his force of personality and reputation for justice to persuade them to return to peaceful pursuits. Miles' plan at first envisaged chasing down Geronimo and his band as criminals; ultimately he was forced to negotiate with Geronimo but on terms very much different from those offered by Crook. Miles transferred all Geronimo's kinsmen living peacefully on the reservation to Florida and then made Geronimo's transfer there a basis for his surrender. The transfer robbed the hostiles of a haven of rest, and, more important, it dried up their source of recruits. In the end it proved to be the most potent argument for Geronimo's surrender.

But Geronimo first had to be run down. The principal expedition for accomplishing this was placed in the hands of Captain Henry Lawton. Like Miles, Lawton did not attend West Point. He entered the Civil War as a volunteer officer, accepted a commission in the regular Army after the war, and was a veteran of several Indian campaigns. He was respected throughout the Army as a practical field soldier and a highly competent commander. An imposing figure at six feet four inches and 230 pounds, Lawton

10

was noted for just those characteristics that were required to carry out Miles' capture and destroy policy: physical endurance and dogged determination. Lawton's sole weakness seems to have been his strong taste for liquor, not uncommon among frontier soldiers. But alcohol turned Lawton into a raging tyrant, a condition which interfered with the performance of his duties.[15] He had little patience, however, with subordinate officers who drank to excess. During the Geronimo campaign he dismissed one of his lieutenants and sent him back to Fort Huachuca charged with misconduct on account of drunkenness.[16] Yet, there is much evidence that Lawton himself did some hard drinking during the campaign and that Wood and others saved his career more than once by smoothing over his drunken rages.[17]

The veteran captain started on the expedition with mixed emotions. Failure to capture the cunning Indians would certainly cloud his prospects for promotion in the Army. On the other hand, success would greatly please Miles, and undoubtedly Lawton's star would rise along with his ambitious commander's. The potential for success in this one campaign spurred him on when the capture of the Indians seemed imminent but at the same time sent him into fits of depression when capture seemed impossible. Lugubrious letters to his wife during the campaign painfully reveal a man who saw his military career resting on the decisions and movements of a group of unpredictable renegade Indians.[18]

III

At the time Miles arrived, Leonard Wood, who had been at Fort Huachuca almost a year, had become both physically and mentally acclimated to life on the frontier. He was stocky with wide, powerful shoulders and arms, a large head and short neck—all of which made him appear taller than his five feet eleven inches. His New England childhood had toughened his physical fiber, and during his life he had almost made a fetish of physical condition. Even in medical school he had kept his body in superb physical condition by running every day and by participating in strenuous athletic activities. His duties on a frontier army post had simply strengthened an already strong body.

While most men saw life on a frontier post as alternating between isolated boredom and exhausting, dangerous Indian expeditions, Wood viewed it as an adventure. Proud of his solid physique and natural endurance and determined to show everyone that he was more than just a "pill roller"—that he was capable of staying with the toughest veteran—the young doctor readily volunteered for all field duty. Because most officers wisely avoided Indian expeditions as much as possible, there was no lack of opportunity for the energetic young doctor. In fact, the day after his arrival at Fort Huachuca in July 1885, Wood accompanied Lawton and Troop B on an Apache expedition. That first day out he rode 30 miles. He admitted to his brother, perhaps with considerable understatement, that he was "feeling a little stiff." Yet he could not conceal his excitement about being out on a field expedition:

> We left Huachuca yesterday morning and came directly over the mountains by a trail which I do not believe you would think a horse could crawl. It was so steep and rocky. In fact, the mountains here are solid rock and with now and then a tree. Part of the way the road wound through a beautiful canyon at the bottom of which was a little stream surrounded by willows from each side of which mountains rose about 2,000 ft., almost straight up. . . . I rode second in line and the Capt. whooped her up a little in some tough places to see how I took them.[19]

Moreover, Wood had concluded that his career lay in the Regular Army rather than in the Medical Corps. These expeditions gave him the opportunity to gain experience as a line officer.

This first expedition lasted two weeks; it was only one of many the young doctor was to embark upon with Lawton and Troop B in the first year at Huachuca. They all ended in much the same way—the Apaches simply melted into the vast stretches of the Sierra Madre Mountains. Although the expeditions discouraged the authorities, the mere chase was exhilarating to Wood: "We chased those Indians for about 200 miles. During the run they changed horses 4 times and managed to keep a good lead. A pretty rough ride. . . ."[20]

When Miles began organizing the campaign against Geronimo, Wood told him, perhaps with a bit of exaggerated optimism, that despite the common belief, the "right sort of white men" could beat the Indians at their own game. Miles, obviously impressed with the cocky spirit of the young contract surgeon, assigned Wood as medical officer to Lawton's expedition.[21]

The expedition, composed of Lawton's Troop B, 4th Cavalry (less, as Wood notes, "a few old noncommissioned officers"), and a company of the 8th infantry under Lieutenant Henry Johnson, differed in composition from the ones sent out by Crook. Twenty Apache scouts were assigned to the expedition, but their activity was to be limited to guiding and trailing; the regular cavalry and infantry formed the main body and striking force of this contingent.[22] Whether even picked frontier veterans could follow the Apache through the desolate Sierra Madre Mountains for an indefinite time was doubtful. Wood was certain they could, Lawton was determined to try, and Miles had no alternative but to order it.

The expedition moved out on May 5, 1886, marching southwestward toward the border town of Nogales. Depredations by at least a portion of Geronimo's band had been reported in the area. Two days later the forces picked up the hostiles' trail leading into the Sonora Province of Mexico. After a short conference with Miles at Nogales, they crossed the border into Mexico, but the expected march into the Sierras did not materialize. After moving about twenty miles into Mexico, the Indians they were trailing (probably only a portion of the larger band) struck southwest, and then, on the nineteenth, moved directly northward back into

Arizona. It was evident, as Wood suggested in his journal entry on May 21, that the Indians were attempting to throw off the expedition from the main body. With no other leads, Lawton moved his small force after them into Arizona, crossing the border near Calabasas.

At Calabasas, Miles came down to confer with Lawton on May 22 and 23. Wood does not record the topic of conversation, but it was obvious that the Indians Lawton was following were not the main band. The hostiles' return to Arizona was only a diversionary tactic, and left both Miles and Lawton undecided as to the next course of action. Apparently no decision was made until five days later when Lawton picked up the trail leading north. He was directed by Miles to follow it. The trail led to a point about fifty miles directly north of Fort Huachuca, where the Indians again turned south and quickly reentered Mexico. Lawton, now convinced that the Indians were striking for the wilds of the Sierra Madre, halted his expedition on June 1 near Calabasas and began collecting supplies and refitting his forces for a long march into Mexico.

During most of June, the expedition's pursuit pattern was virtually set. The Indians were constantly on the move, using every diversionary tactic, including setting fire to the entire countryside, to throw off their pursuers. The twenty scouts were used primarily to track the Indians, and although they were amazingly effective in keeping the expedition on the trail, the expedition never laid eyes on the band of hostiles from the beginning of the pursuit until the surrender of Geronimo in August.

Especially after entering Mexico, where hard information was scarce, tracking the Indians became a matter of intuition. Even when the trail was fairly clear, Lawton was never certain whether he was following the main band or some splinter group that had broken away to throw them off. Much of the time the expedition was totally ignorant of the exact whereabouts of the hostiles. Acting on the scantiest information, several times they marched twenty-five or thirty miles, ending up within five miles of their original point of departure without ever knowing for certain that they had been following the Indians. It was a mild foretaste of the extreme frustration and discouragement the members of the expedition were to experience after they plunged into Mexico for the second time.

Wood was in Fort Huachuca gathering supplies when Lawton struck south across the border. By this time his role as medical officer to the expedition had become secondary. He now served as Lawton's principal aide, as indicated by his assignment to lead a packtrain from Calabasas to the command, which was rapidly pursuing the Indians into Sonora. By force marching for three days and far into each night, Wood managed to overtake Lawton on June 16. Wood's first experience at command was a noticeable success. It indicated not only how naturally he took command responsibility, but also how much about field service he had learned during his year on the frontier. Later, when one officer after another dropped by the side, Lawton felt quite confident in giving command of the infantry company to Wood.

During the rest of June and all of July the expedition pushed deeper and deeper into Mexico and the Sierra Madre. Wood's description of the daily marches through the desolate country needs no amplification. Day after day in scorching heat (the temperature rising to 120 degrees), beset by insects of all kinds and constantly forced to vary their march in search of water, the expedition pursued an elusive and unpredictable enemy. The Indians left little or no trail, and what they left was frequently destroyed by a cloudburst or covered over by Mexican irregulars who were also chasing the hostiles. Compelled to follow a trail on the flimsiest of evidence, the expedition frequently lost contact with the main band. But somehow the sharp senses of the Apache scouts allowed the expedition to remain in the general vicinity of Geronimo's band.

On July 13 undetected, they came up on Geronimo's camp near the Arros River. They prepared to surprise him in camp, but while maneuvering to surround him and prevent his escape, the command was discovered and the Indians fled, leaving behind food, clothing, and horses. The reaction after the excitement of an expected fight left the command thoroughly exhausted and demoralized. For a brief moment the Indians had been within their grasp; now they had vanished again, Lawton knew not where. For two weeks afterward the expedition floundered around the area in search of the Indians' trail, crossing and recrossing the Arros and Yaqui Rivers, swollen by almost daily thunderstorms. The morale of the expedition sank to a new low. Lawton, always skeptical but still determined, began to lose hope. Their failure to capture the Indians on July 13 broke his will. In dismay he wrote his wife that he would "cry if it would do any good." His hopes for an advancement out of this campaign seemed lost, for "Gen'l. Miles will be terribly disappointed and will probably think I have been careless or negligent, and we have worked *so hard* and under such trying circumstances, it seems too bad to fail. . . ."[23] He began to question whether the expedition was wise after all: "I think it would have been better to have stopped operations during this month and August as it is really too hot to do anything; to attempt to work is only a farce."[24]

To add to his troubles, Wood was bitten by a tarantula. With either a foolish stubbornness or the knowledge of how much Lawton depended on him, Wood insisted on bearing his share of the work. When the bite became swollen and feverish, he simply lanced it and kept marching. It was a kind of foolhardy bravado which, as a doctor he should have known, could have ended his life. Finally Lawton, certain that Wood was going to kill himself, ordered a travois made to drag Wood to some nearby ranch. To Lawton this was the final blow: "I am almost broken up with misfortune," he complained to his wife. "It not only leaves the command without a medical officer, but no one to look after him, and he has always been my warmest friend and supporter. I don't know what I shall do without him. It seems as though I were having misfortune after misfortune."[25]

Just as the expedition seemed hopelessly doomed, a series of events rescued it. Wood miraculously recovered from the bite, which considerably raised Lawton's spirits. More important, on August 3, Lieutenant James Parker, in command of H Troop, 4th Cavalry, appeared at Lawtons' camp on the Nacori Creek, bringing with him Lieutenant Charles Gatewood with a new policy from Miles. Rather than treating the Indians as fugitives, Miles, obviously discouraged at the expedition's inability to capture or destroy Geronimo, had decided to try Crook's methods. He had sent Gatewood, who was known and respected by the Apaches, to begin negotiations. Lawton's orders were to put Gatewood in contact with Geronimo, a sizable problem in itself since catching him had been Lawton's chief aim from the start of the campaign.

The appearance of Gatewood, one of Crook's men, with orders to negotiate, virtually acknowledged the expedition's failure to accomplish its original goal. Lawton at first balked; it was difficult to admit defeat after they had gone through so much.[26] But then, apparently realizing the serious condition of the expedition, Lawton ordered his men out in all directions to find Geronimo's trail. "I am pretty tired," he wrote his wife, "and feel the strain of responsibility weighing on me." Whether he agreed with the change of policy or not, Lawton was still convinced that his future in the Army lay with "the action of General Miles and his approval or disapproval. . . ."[27] If Miles wanted to negotiate, he would do his best to find Geronimo.

The scouts found the trail leading north toward Arizona and Lawton immediately sent Gatewood ahead with ten picked men. Gatewood's Indians caught up with the band some three weeks later and Geronimo agreed to parlay with Miles' representative. His band was dead tired. They had eluded Lawton's expedition these past few weeks only by keeping constantly on the move. To add to their troubles, on the trip northward a contingent of Mexican irregulars struck their trail. Capture by this peasant militia meant almost certain execution. In short, if given acceptable terms, Geronimo was ready to surrender to the Americans.

But Miles' terms, as explained by Gatewood, were harsh: the hostiles were to agree to be transferred with their families to Florida; otherwise the Army would pursue them indefinitely. Geronimo demurred; he wanted to be sent back to the reservation in Arizona. Gatewood, who had never had much confidence in the mission, who was sick and wanted to get back to civilization, was ready to admit defeat. But by this time Lawton was committed to the plan. Moreover, he was certain that Geronimo was anxious to surrender or else he would never have entered into conversations with Gatewood in the first place. Lawton goaded Gatewood on.[28] Gatewood's next meeting with Geronimo was more successful and the Indian leader agreed to march north with the expedition to meet with Miles and further discuss the terms of surrender.

The campaign appeared to be over. But just on this brink of success, a new development threatened to send the expedition plunging once again in the mountain wilderness. A company of Mexican irregulars who had recently taken up the chase moved within striking range of Lawton's force and Geronimo's nearby camp. The sight of the Mexicans threw the Indians into a state of extreme excitement. Even the expedition began throwing up breastworks in preparation for a fight. It was undoubtedly true, as Wood wrote in his journal, that some of the soldier's hoped to "even up with the Mexicans for poor Crawford's death." But Lawton, determined not to allow this threat to destroy the mission at the eleventh hour, sent Wood out to meet with the Mexicans. It was in an almost identical incident that Crawford was shot, and no doubt Crawford's death hung heavily in Wood's thoughts as he approached the Mexican contingent. Dressed in a "pair of canton flannel drawers, and an old blouse, a pair of moccasins and a hat without a crown," Wood did not exude authority. Nevertheless, the Mexicans listened as he explained that the Indians had surrendered to the American Army and were therefore in military custody. Any trouble, he told them, would find the soldiers fighting alongside Geronimo's Indians. Although in an ugly mood and extremely anxious to fall upon the Indians in revenge for their many depredations, the Mexican leader, the prefect of Arispe, saw the futility of such an attack. The danger passed, but it convinced Lawton more than ever that he must get the Indians out of Mexico and into the hands of Miles.

Finally, Miles arrived on September 3 at Skeleton Canyon in Southern Arizona. After several days of conference he concluded an agreement with Geronimo: the hostiles surrendered with the understanding that they would be sent to Florida to join their relatives. On September 8 the Indians were put aboard a special train at Fort Bowie and dispatched to Fort Marion, Florida. The historic expedition was over.

The expedition had been on the trail continuously for four months with scarcely any rest, marching a total of 3,041 miles over the wildest, most rugged country in North America. Thirty Indians had consumed the time, energy, and material of more than two thousand soldiers. When it was over, as one writer had observed, "they had not been defeated, they had been subjugated; they had made peace as one belligerent power makes peace with another, on terms acceptable to both."[29]

Although the Lawton expedition successfully ended the threat of Apache depredation in the Southwest, its original aim of capturing or destroying Geronimo's band with the "right sort of white man" was never realized. They never found the right sort of white man who could remain on the trail throughout the campaign. The composition of the expedition changed constantly as the men became exhausted or sick and were relieved. Several times whole units were replaced by fresh troops. Only Wood and Lawton served the entire campaign. Perhaps other white men could have equalled Wood's and Lawton's feat, but Miles never sent them.

Other factors than physical endurance caused the surrender of Geronimo. They were the same reasons for the ultimate defeat of the Indians in other parts of the West: the superior manpower and material resources behind the expedition, the hostility of

19

the native inhabitants, and the tendency of the Indians to run rather than fight pitched battles from favorable defensive positions. In fact, when the wilderness of the Sierra Madre Mountains equalized the two forces, the Indians clearly emerged superior, as evidenced by the floundering of the expedition in the Arros River basin. It was knowing that the American government had the resources to chase them for an indefinite period of time, rather than the threat of capture, that brought about the surrender of Geronimo's band.

On the other hand, if the American soldier was no match for the Indian in the latter's natural habitat, the expedition did prove that the Apache could no longer safely conceal himself in the fastnesses of the Sierra Madre Mountains. The expedition showed that a unit of American soldiers could at least exist in the wilderness of northern Mexico. At its deepest penetration it became in effect a counter-guerrilla force. Cut loose from their ties with outside resources, the soldiers foraged for some of their food (or at least for enough of a variety to keep them well), adapted themselves to the wilderness by dressing in Indian style of a brief outer garment (issue underwear) and moccasins. So well did the soldiers acclimate themselves to the environment, the natives frequently mistook them for Indians. Thus, the expedition had the positive effect of showing that a regular army contingent could adjust to the rigors of guerrilla warfare sufficiently to threaten the safe existence of hostile Indians.

IV

Almost immediately after the capture of Geronimo and his band an intense public controversy arose over who should get the credit for the capture of Geronimo—Miles or Crook; over the loyalty or disloyalty of Apache scouts; over the disposition of Geronimo's band after capture. Charges and counter-charges filled official and unofficial channels, and ultimately most of the main participants published their interpretations of the campaign. Shortly after the campaign, an apology by Crook appeared in the *Journal of Military Service Institute*.[30] A few years later (1891), John G. Bourke, one of Crook's aides, published *On the Border with Crook*,[31] the first major account sympathetic with Crook's methods. Miles entered the controversy-in-print in 1896 with the publication of his *Personal Recollections* and in 1911 reviewed the campaign again in *Serving The Republic*.[32] Needless to say, Miles did not lose the opportunity to extol his policies at the expense of Crook's. Miles' two books, plus the appearance of an autobiography by James Parker,[33] an admirer of Miles, called forth a new apology for Crook's methods from Britton Davis, Crook's most trusted and loyal aide.[34] Davis was supposed to have remarked that he was so "tired of hearing so many untruths about Geronimo and his capture that I sat down and wrote the truth about it. . . ."[35] But like most other participants, Davis had a cause to serve. His *Truth About Geronimo* does shed further light on the Geronimo campaign, but it does not have the finality the title implies.

The Wood journal may be considered a part of the continuing controversy. Wood was a Miles man. Miles chose him for the campaign and generously rewarded him afterward. Throughout the campaign Wood believed that the expedition of which he was a part was an attempt to do what the Crook men said could not be done. While he did not become directly involved in the controversy, his sympathies clearly lay with Miles' policy.

But Wood's account is much more than simply a defense of Miles. It has much wider historical significance as a contribution to our knowledge of Indian fighting on the southwestern frontier. Even if the young Leonard Wood did find a sense of personal excitement in the campaign, what emerges from the journal is no romantic tale of adventure. As the journal clearly shows, Indian pacification for the Regular Army in the Southwest was a dirty, brutal undertaking, involving raw physical hardship that placed a premium on a soldier's courage and endurance. While the Lawton expedition was unique in its conclusion—Geronimo's downfall was "an event of enormous significance in the history of the Southwest"[36]—its experiences were by no means unusual. They were repeated daily by the Regular Army in the Southwest. Wood's graphic description of these experiences helps us to better understand the Army's constabulary role in Indian pacification.

Part I: *Organizing the Expedition*

Chapter 1: *"The Right Sort of White Men"*

"I told [General Miles] I believed the right sort of white
men could eventually break these Indians up and compel
them to surrender."

Leonard Wood Diary, entry May 4, 1886.

We are about to leave on an expedition. . . . We are
going down into the hot lands of Northern Mexico and
into the rough unknown Sierra Madre Mountains. . . .
It is Miles' great effort to do what General Crook failed
to do."

Wood to Jake, May 5, 1886.

May 4, 1886

Ever since the original outbreak of Geronimo and
Natchez, a more or less active campaign has been waged against
them. The last phase of the campaign has involved the station-
ing all along the frontier at the water holes and main passes of
detachments of troops, in the hopes of thus embarrassing the
Apaches, getting prompt news of their movements, and being
able to follow them either into Mexico or the United States. This
campaign, as a rule, proved unavailing, the Indians slipping
through the cordon, broken in many places as it is by long
stretches of country, 30, 40, or even 50 miles in extent. Activity
has gradually diminished, and it has become evident that nothing
will be accomplished in this way. Several expeditions have been
sent into Mexico; one of them under Captain [Wirt] Davis, 4th
Cavalry; another under Captain [Emmet] Crawford, who was

25

killed in a fight with Mexicans south of Nacori.[1] One of these expeditions established contact with the Indians, and brought them to the frontier. The conference here was only partially successful, a number of the Indians, including Geronimo and Natchez, and a considerable portion of the hardest fighting bucks, with their families, breaking out and going back to Mexico. General Crook was relieved in the Spring, having become, I believe, thoroughly discouraged as to the results. Colonel Shafter,[2] 1st Infantry, stated that General Crook had said in his presence that these Indians could not be caught in 20 years.

Brigadier General Nelson A. Miles was assigned to the command of the department on General Crook's relief, and on assuming command determined to organize several expeditions, lightly equipped, and composed of thoroughly efficient officers and men, with a view to running these Indians down. Captain Henry W. Lawton, Troop B, 4th Cavalry, has been assigned to command the principal expedition. I saw General Miles at Fort Bowie[3] and had a long talk with him. I told him I believed the right sort of white men could eventually break these Indians up and compel them to surrender. I have been selected as medical officer of the expedition.

The expedition will consist of Troop B, 4th Cavalry, less a few old non-commissioned officers and men on detached service; a detachment of Worth's and Bailey's companies of the 8th Infantry, with a few men from another company under the command of Lieut. Henry Johnson, 8th Infantry; a detachment of 30 San Carlos and White Mountain Apache Indian Scouts, under Lieut. Leighton Finley, 10th U. S. Cavalry; two packtrains under William Brown and Daly,[4] packers, which will furnish the pack transportation. Relay packtrains will be kept in touch with the command by means of special couriers and will bring forward supplies from time to time, so that the command will not be delayed waiting for supplies. These trains will be furnished with small, but sufficient, escorts. Everything has been stripped down to the limit and an effort will be made to keep the hostiles constantly on the move and eventually force them to surrender. There is a good deal of feeling between the partisans of General Crook and the friends of General Miles.[5]

A rather quiet day at the post today.[6] The infantry command moved out under Lieutenant Johnson. I went out with him to put on the trail for the Tevis Ranch,[7] on the Barbacomara. Went out about 5 miles with him, pointed out the trail, and returned to the post. Did some packing, and preparing my quarters for a long absence. Rode about 10 miles horseback today.[8] The horse assigned to me, a flea-bitten grey, called "Baby," killed his last rider. Had a hard time with him today.

May 5th, 1886

The Command, consisting of the Cavalry, Indian Scouts, and packtrains, left the post this morning. I pulled out about an hour after the command, and marched to Elgin Station.[9] Packtrains got off the road on the way down. Stopped en route to see an old patient of mine by the name of Hand, who had a very badly broken leg, compound comminutated fracture of the thigh. Going to get a good result, with only about ½ or ¾ of an inch shortening. Left instructions for his further care.[10] Distance marched today 15 miles. Command busy today getting things knocked into shape, packs adjusted to the mules, and things shaken down for the long march. Have with us two alleged guides named Allsup and Ames, both frontier bummers. Ames discharged today for lying; nearly ruined his horse.

May 6th, 1886

Marched to a point about three miles below Crittendon,[11] where camp was established for the night. Lawton and I returned to Crittendon to get supplies which have been sent down by train. Dr. Paul Brown, post surgeon, came down on the train with some supplies, also Contract Surgeon Terrill. Marched 18 miles. Our camp was at the head of a small creek to the left of the railroad, going over, about three miles below the town.

May 7th, 1886

Marched to McCullough's ranch on the Santa Cruz River. Had a rather comfortable march. Command gradually shaking into shape. Infantry joined us yesterday. After making camp, Lawton rode into Nogales,[12] for dispatches. Total distance marched today 24 miles. We received word at Nogales to wait for General Miles who was en route to Nogales and wishes to go over the details of the campaign with Captain Lawton. Drs. Brown and Terrill went on to Nogales last night, for the purpose of attending to Corporal Scott, of Captain [T. C.] Lebo's Troop,[13] 10th Cavalry, who was badly shot in the fight near the Santa Barbara peaks. They amputated his thigh today. We remained in town all night. Dr. Terrill distinguished himself by getting pretty full. General Miles arrived this afternoon and had a long conference with Captain Lawton.

May 8th, 1886

Captain Lawton, Dr. Brown and I went out to camp early, and the command marched to a ranch on the Santa Cruz River, distance 25 miles. Lawton and I then went on to the Mescatel Ranch to see Captain Lebo and Lieutenant Powhattan Clark [sic][14], whom we found in camp there. This gave us an additional 12 miles, making a total for us of 37 miles for the day. Also found one of Lawton's sergeants, who had been sent on with despatches to Lebo, and one man, waiting for us. Had the details of Lebo's fight from Lt. Clark and himself. They ran into the Apaches in a very strong position in a tongue of broken lava-like rock, where the cover was perfect, and the troop had a very hard time getting them out. One or two men killed, Corporal Scott and others badly wounded. Lebo distinguished himself by great coolness and courage. The whole affair seems to have been a very pretty piece of work. Returned to camp in the evening.

Command 25   Officers 37

Organizing the Expedition

May 9th, 1886

Captain Lawton sent me early this morning to San Lazaro to buy of a Major Ruiz 3,000 pounds of barley, at 2-3/7¢ per pound. Private Roland went with me. Pack train came up for the grain and we all waited there until its arrival, then went on to the Rincon Ranch, and from there on to a camp 2 miles from where Benson is in camp. Lawton and I rode up to his camp and returned later in the afternoon. Total distance today, 35 miles. The Indians who had the fight with Lebo have struck South into Sonora, crossing over the Las Pinas mountains. Weather pretty hot. Had dinner in camp today, and everyone sat around in the boiling sun with the perspiration running off like water.

May 10, 1886

Changed our camp into an adjoining canon where the water supply was better. [Lt. H. C.] Benson joined us with a detachment of the men of the Troop, B, [4th Cavalry] which he has been in command of for the last few days. He joined our command at 12:45. The men under Benson, thoroughly demoralized by bad handling, too much demanded of the men.[15] Captain Lawton, Lt. Johnson, Lt. Finley, and I, started out with 12 dismounted cavalrymen, 19 infantrymen, and 30 scouts, 3 packers, 14 mules, 10 packs, on the Indian Trail, which Benson gave us some information about, having been on it for a time. We struck the trail 5 miles from camp and followed it for four hours, when we lost it in the dry rock country on top of the mountains, and went into camp.

In the meantime the Indians had gone on to locate the trail. The cause of losing it was largely due to Mexican troops having passed over it ahead of us and cutting it up badly. A frightful country; the ridges are right up and down. The whole mountains are on fire. Fire evidently set by the Indians. Fires are all about us tonight. The Indians set these forest fires to cover the trail and to delay us as much as possible. We put out the fires and set back fires on all sides near our camp, as the heat was becoming tremendous. Animals badly frightened. The air is full of immense swarms of insects flying from the flames. We camped near a small pool of water only a few feet long and 4 or 5 inches deep, formed by a seepage from the rocks. The camp is in a canon 400 or 500 feet deep, the mountains rising up on all sides. Dense heavy clouds of smoke in camp. Had nothing to sleep on tonight except a roll of leaves and a poncho for cover. Our back fires have been successful, and we have a few acres about us free from fire. The heat has been tremendous. Distance marched today about 9 miles. The rations are hardtack and bacon, and little else.[16] Country exceedingly rough.

May 11th, 1886

Captain Lawton's mule went off last night, strayed. Took the back trail. This morning sent an Indian back to camp for her. Four Indians whom we sent out to locate the trail, returned after a few hours, and we got off at 9:00 A.M. Followed the trail over very rough country for 10 or 12 miles. Many hills, almost perpendicular, and it was difficult to get the packs over them. Was on foot with the advance, consisting of 2 or 3 dismounted cavalrymen and 4 or 5 Indians, most of the day. The hostile Apache trail led off from near our camp to the right, up a steep canon for about 2 miles, then over some rough mountains to another deep canon. We found two dead horses on the north side of the mountain, and struck the hostile camp on the south side, where they had evidently stopped for a day or possibly more. The trail leading to and from this camp was very heavy and plainly marked, and just south of the camp on the outleading trail a heavy horse trail came in, evidently several days fresher than that from the camp. Went out after deer in order to get something for a change.[17] Did not get any. Indians picked up a couple. While coming in ran into two couriers coming to our camp with despatches, but they had nothing of importance. One came in on a cavalry horse which was pretty nearly done up.

The Indians on their return from hunting reported having found two dead bodies in the canon about 5 miles from here. Distance marched today 10 miles.

During my hunt today saw some grass shacks in a canon. Very carefully approached them and found them to be located on a little creek. In the bed of the stream lay 5 dead Mexicans, bodies beginning to swell. Evidently killed a day or two ago. Miners. Killed by Apaches. Saw some shells in the grass. It is evident they were shot from only a few yards away. One of the bodies powder-burned. In addition to the march made by the troops, made about 8 miles on my hunting trip. Total distance 18 miles.

Troops 10-12   Myself 18

May 12th, 1886

Left camp at 5:45 A.M., marched down the main canon in which we camped last night for about 2 miles, then struck across country to the bodies which the Indians found, which were on the main trail. Found the bodies in a very rough country. Marched down the canon in which we found them for ½ mile, then came a split in the trail, the main stock trail went to the left on the ridge, a small foot trail went on down the canon. We followed the main trail. Marching hard and rough. Indians picked up a couple of deer, which we ate on the spot as we were all hungry.[18] Went on down to the Magdalena to a point 9 miles above Imuras [Imuris], Sonora. About 3 miles after striking the ridge we came upon an old camp, and in it we found the remains of an old hat, a woman's, and some pieces of white cloth, old pony shoes of rawhide, and other evidences of the Indian camp. On leaving this camp the trail scattered for about 100 yards, and then seemed to come all together again. Lawton thinks there must have been a large party leaving the trail, and suspects that it may have been covered by a broad trail made by dragging a dead horse or other body down the mountainside. Indians do not think so, as a rule.

Just before reaching the Magdalena River the trail ran into a

31

large draw and became obscured by the thousands of horses and cattle tracks, with which this valley is swarming. Upon reaching camp with the cavalry and Indians, the Infantry and packs being about an hour behind, Captain Lawton and I went down to a ranch about a mile down the river and succeeded in buying about 600 pounds of green wheat straw, at about 1¢ per pound. Also a young steer for $15.00. We also ran into a gang of section hands, and made an arrangement to go down to Imuris and communicate with General Miles. The section hands are to take us down on a hand car.[19] Expect to return on the morning train, reaching here about 2:30 A.M. Lt. Finley and Lawton left camp at 3:00 P.M. for Imuris.

The Indians under Finley will go out tomorrow to look for the trail, which seems to be leading west by south. Captain Lawton does not wish to cross the railroad without orders from General Miles. One packtrain is at our old camp near Rincon, except 9 packs, which we have with us. One man of Johnson's command gave out today and I sent him in. All the large canons in the Pintas have some water. Our present camp is on rather low damp ground. Marched today 15 miles. Have a frightful case of poison oak. The relics of a woman's hat, etc., found in the camp, are believed to be those belonging to the Peck child, the little daughter of a Mr. and Mrs. Peck, whose ranch was jumped by Apaches a few weeks ago. The mother was outraged and killed, and the father tied up to a tree, the Indians intending to torture him, but he became violently crazy and they turned him loose. This little girl is still with her captors, a child about 12 years old.[20]

May 13, 1886

Captain Lawton and Finley returned about 3:00 A.M. today. Train stopped and let them off near the camp. A quiet day in camp. Washed out clothes. Finley with 17 Indians out looking up the trail, one of the civilian couriers is with him. One was sent to Lt. Benson to bring on the packtrain and balance of the command. A good many Mexicans in camp today.

Lt. Finley returned about 3:30 P.M. with the report that the trails were scattered much on crossing the railroad, and that they united in several large trails a few miles west of the railroad, and that one small trail led northwest, but that the main trail led southwest and presented signs which the Indians say indicate that the squaws and the great portion of the bucks are with this party. During the day Finley's party picked up several horses abandoned by the Indians. Have received orders to take the train to Imuris tonight to get off some despatches and see about forwarding grain. Poison oak somewhat better.

May 14th, 1886

Took the train at 12:40 A.M. and went down to Imuris. Met a man, a nephew of Bill Nye, on the train. He is on his way down to Hermocillo. Got something to eat at the station and bunked in with the telegraph operator, who was very drunk, and the bed was rather small. This man was named Montgomery, evidently sent here by mistake as he spoke no Spanish. Messages were coming in in Spanish, which he could not read, so he sent out uniformly the following: Go to Hell, I don't speak Spanish. In the morning I met a Mister Tedayo, whom I first saw last summer on the Cananea Ranch. He very kindly assisted me in securing forage, etc. Got some things at the store, and at 2 P.M. started back to camp, my transportation having turned up. Many reports of fighting in the Altar district, west of the railroad. Montoya, a Mexican who speaks Indian and Apache, and has been the Apache interpreter at San Carlos, is going to join our command from Magdalena.

Struck the trail of the command going south. Followed it to camp near the Barbasac Ranch, where we were very kindly treated. We alarmed them very much, as they took us for Indians. Couriers came in announcing the arrival, or expected arrival, of Scout Chimney[21] and Corporal Ryan. Four horses obtained at the ranch and Lt. Finley and Scout Dick,[22] 1st sergeant of the Apache Scouts, went out after them. Returned near morning. The old Senora who owns this property is quite ill. Gave her some medicine. It is a fine old place, and the home of a family which has in the past furnished several governors of the province. The place is, for a Mexican ranch, well kept up. There is a good stream running through it, and the land is rich and well tilled. Made altogether today about 30 miles on horseback.

May 15th, 1886

Made a very rapid march to Mohonara Ranch, the same one where I stopped last year when I was out with Hatfield's[23] command. On the march we came up with the scouts. Made the trip today on foot and came in as the first white man into camp. On arriving at the camp learned from the Mexicans that the hostiles were at the Ojo de Agua last night. The cause of moving our camp yesterday while I was at Imuris was due to the report received from Lt. Bill Davis,[24] 10th Cavalry, who is in this section with a command. His report was to the effect that he struck fresh Indian trail and freshly killed horses yesterday, trail leading toward the east. We marched up to the mission near the ruined town of Opoto and camped, reaching there about 5:30. Purchased 100 bundles of green straw forage. In the evening we went down to a ranch 2 miles below and heard some very good Yaqui music. Distance marched today 25 miles.

May 16th, 1886

Captain Lawton and Finley went out with the Indians to look for the trail. Benson and I remained in the camp. In the afternoon couriers came in and brought a letter to go to Malpais Ranch, 15 miles northeast from here, to overtake the Indians who were with Captain Lawton and Finley. The order was complied with, and we went into camp 3 miles below an old smelter.

Lt. R. A. Brown,[25] 4th Cavalry, with I Troop, came in. Dr. George Andrews is with him. This command reported fresh trail; that they had jumped an Indian camp during the day, getting a number of saddles. Total distance marched 13 miles.

May 17th, 1886

Brown left this morning, and we took a hot trail about 9 miles from camp, and followed it over very rough country, running down to San Lazaro. Met Hatfield with his troop and Dorst's troop, under Cook.[26] Left them, and camped near Rincon. Distance marched today, 25 miles.

May 18th, 1886

Struck a hot trail this morning, a continaution of the one we were on yesterday. Indians expecting a fight momentarily. Saw a large bear. Found a number of freshly killed cattle, and recovered a good many abandoned horses. Captain Lawton says he saw 16 and more later on, 30 in all.

Found a number of camps, one with the fire burning and pieces of meat still smouldering. Country very rough and dry. The trail passed near the Santa Barbara Peaks. The men are all pretty well played out; Captain Lawton and Lieutenant Finley were mounted all day. Benson and I walked. Went into camp about 4 P.M. after 9 hours of constant marching. Passed water three times. Total distance marched 25 miles. Country passed over today has been very rough.

May 19th, 1886

Left camp very early this morning, at 4:20 A.M., and marched with the Indians for a number of miles, leading my horse. About 8 A.M. we struck the railroad and found traces of a killing in the shape of a dead horse, shot, and two pools of blood, trail crossing the railroad track. Captain Lawton and I, with Corporal Ryan and 3 men, went north on the trail along the track about 5 miles, where we met a few men of the Sonora Land

Company, and learned that 2 men were killed where we found the pools of blood. The time of the killing was yesterday afternoon, so we must have been on a very hot trail yesterday. Bodies were removed yesterday.

The troops and Indians continued on the trail while we were off on this mission, after which we cut obliquely across country and cut the trail about 3 miles from the railroad, and then followed it about 5 or 6 miles further before overtaking the troops, who were camped on top of a ridge. Stopped a short time to scout through some neighboring canons for water, but I found none fit for use. While looking about came on several burros with saddles on, so that we supposed someone had been killed near here, but found later on in the day that they belonged to Mexicans who saw our Scouts, mistook them for Indians, and abandoned their mounts, taking to the mountains.

From this point we went into some very rough country and finally into one much rougher than any we have thus far struck, full of canons and scarcely any water at all. About 5:30 P.M. we began to hunt for water and finally got into the canon of the Rio de las Planchas de la Plata and followed it down three miles, reaching water about 2 miles above the little town of Las Planchas de La Plata. We went into camp here, all rather tired and the stock well used up from thirst and hard climbing. Finley rode his little mule all day, doing no work on foot.[27] Montoya has worn down three horses of his own, and is now engaged in killing one of the troop horses.

After reaching camp I went down to the town, a miserable little collection of Mexican houses with several small smelters and one or two degenerate Americans hanging around. At the small store I got a few things, such as canned peaches, pieces of chocolate and 3 cans of oysters which had been for many years away from the ocean. The people there fixed me up a supper of carne seca,[28] also some boiled milk, a little tea, with dried apple sauce. It is needless to say that it was appreciated. Just as I was sitting down to it Lawton and Finley came down and helped me out, and we all went back to camp. Our horses were about used up for want of water and everyone made a rush for it as soon as we struck it. Lawton hired a Mexican guide today, and also sent another to meet the packtrain at Agua Seca and turn them this way to our camp. The civilian courier, Wilson, was sent out last night to bring them to Agua Seca. Total distance marched today 35 miles.

May 20th, 1886

Captain Lawton and Lt. Finley with a few Indians went out this morning to look for the trail. Benson and I went down to town to get some rations, anything we could find, flour, beans, and salt. Absent from camp only a short time; on return did a little reading and wrote up my diary. Slept and idled away the day generally. Walked altogether about 5 miles. Had some fresh beef during the day. Indians fixing up their moccasins and getting ready for hard work. This country is on the edge of the desert lying east of the Gulf of Lower California and south of Tucson. Country dry and treeless. Very little water in the country. Lawton and Finley returned about 3 P.M. and reported trail as leading west through a very rough country.

Lt. [Robert] Walsh turned up in the afternoon and reported packtrain at or near Nogales. Lt. Johnson off again and sent to Huachuca in arrest. This officer has done good work but has repeatedly taken too much whiskey. Relieved today.[29] Benson went to Nogales in the P.M. and returned late at night or early in the morning. Brought in with him Vinton. Made today 5 miles on foot.

May 21st, 1886

Left camp early this morning. Walsh in command of the troop. Benson has gone back to get the packtrain at Agua Seca and take charge of it from now on. Marched all day through a very rough country, about the roughest I have ever seen on a scout. Trail very warm. Very little water on the trail, which was very crooked, winding back and forth. Evidently the Indians are doing their best to throw us off. We marched 25 miles to get ahead 15. Camped about 5 P.M. on Bear Valley, with good water and grass for this country. Found a heavy cavalry trail cutting the Apache trail near camp and rather blinding it. Found 8 men, Infantry, Captain Parker's company, under a sergeant, who tells us that Captain Lebo has just left and is camped near here. Distance marched today 25 miles.

May 22nd, 1886

Indians and Finley went out about 6 A.M. to look for the hostile trail, taking with them Billy Long, civilian courier. About 11 A.M. Long returned, reporting trail leading toward Calabasas. We got off at 12 and cut across country to point where scouts were waiting for us, and from there went on through a very rough country down to the Santa Cruz River, about 1½ miles east of Calabasas[30] and camped there. I left the command about 6 miles from the river and came on ahead, down a rough canon trail to the river, hoping to be able to buy some forage, but could not make it. Met Brown, one of our packers, at the river. He told me General Miles was in town. Captain Lawton came in and we rode up to Calabasas, found the packtrain, also General Miles, Captain Tinsdale, and Dr. Brown there. Distance marched 23 miles.

May 23rd, 1886

In Calabasas all day. Returned to camp quite late last night and camp[ed] up today. Awfully hot, 107 degrees in the shade. Captain Lawton has had a long conference with General Miles.[31] Slept on the hotel verandah last night.

May 24th, 1886

Dr. Brown has been here since the night we got in. A quiet day today. Lawton sick all day with muscular rheumatism. Very hot weather. General Miles and Dapray[32] went to Willcox[33] this morning. Not anything new thus far. Went down to camp in the A.M. Slept in camp. Captain Tisdale slept at the hotel.

May 25th, 1886

A quiet day. Went to the hotel at 9:00 A.M. and remained there until the afternoon. Nothing going on. Just before supper a telegraph message came, ordering us with D, 8th Infantry, 20 Indians, 20 days rations, to proceed to Pantano,[34] a station 30 miles east of Tucson on the Southern Pacific Railroad and near the Rincon Mountains in the Santa Catalina Range, where a man was killed today by hostile Indians. This indicates that a number of the hostiles have gone north either to draw us off from the main body or possibly to work in that country instead of going south. Orders were issued to get everything ready without delay, and we were packed and ready an hour before the special train arrived. Left Calabasas at 11:00 P.M., and after a rather pleasant trip arrived at Pantano about 5:00 A.M.

May 26th, 1886

We found Lt. Bill Davis there, and learned that D and H troops under Lebo were only 4 miles distant. Davis has only 14 horses fit for service and these are much run down and almost worthless. Benson came as far as Huachuca and left us to gather supplies and things needed. Lt. Territt, 8th Infantry, came on with us in command of the Infantry, of which he has been in command since Lt. Johnson's arrest for drunkenness. Dr. [Charles] Barrows came with us as far as Lebo's command, which he joined under orders from Department Headquarters. We breakfasted with Davis and Carter Johnson and then marched over to Lebo's camp, found the trail at that point, followed southwest by west 12 miles to ranch, where we went into camp. It is evident that the Indians have made a short detour in the Santa Catalina Range and then again struck south. The trail ran along the South side of the Santa Catalina Mountains.

39

Camped on good water, but very poor grass. Davis and Johnson came into our camp at 5:30 P.M. and went into camp near us. Made 15 miles today over a very rough dry country.

May 27th, 1886

Left the camp at 6:00 A.M. and marched across country nearly due south to the railroad, and found where the hostiles had broken through the fence at a large swamp 2 miles west of Pantano. Captain Lawton and I went into Pantano and sent telegrams to General Miles announcing the trail, and were directed to investigate it. On our return to camp we found Davis with us to bring back reports concerning direction of trail and any other information which may be useful for Davis to have. Camped at a ranch 9 miles from the railroad near the most northerly spur of the Santa Ritas west of the Total Wreck Mining District.[35] Davidson's ranch.[36] Had supper at the ranch. Got some hay there. We are now 28 miles southwest of Tucson. Marched today 15 miles.

May 28th, 1886

Left camp early and marched southwest, and gradually swung around to the west. Trail leading through the northern portion of the Santa Rita spur and then running down in the plain west of the mountain again. About 30 miles southeast of Tucson and 25 miles from Pantano. Camped at the Amigos smelter. Trail led through a very rough country, most of the day, and was very crooked. Trail very hard to follow and much obscured by cattle tracks, etc. No definite reports of Indians. Our scouts last saw the trail at 4:00 P.M. near the Camp.

May 29th, 1886

Command in camp all day at a mine known as the Columbia smelter, on the west side of the Santa Rita Mountains. Finley and I out with the Indians, looking up trails. Weather warm. Returned about 2:00 P.M. The indications are that the trail runs south, but on it are a number of shod horses, and our Indians are uncertain as to its nature. Captain Lawton tried to secure some citizens to take a message to Pantano, but on account of the report of Indians having cut in behind us they did not wish to go except at an exorbitant price.[37] I told Captain Lawton I would go in with the despatch. Took one man from Territt's command, an old soldier who was about used up. Mounted him on Territt's mule, which was the only available animal. Left camp about 5:00 P.M., and headed for Pantano, distant about 25 miles, but on account of the crookedness of the trail, our losing it in the darkness, etc., the distance was increased probably 5 or 10 miles. The old soldier played out when about ⅔ of the distance in. Pointed out to him the peaks of the mountains east of Tucson, told him to strike north, keeping these peaks somewhat to his left, and when he struck the railroad to turn to the right until he reached Pantano.

I reached Pantano about 10:00 P.M. Found Whispering Bill Davis and Carter Johnson in camp there. Most of their horses broken down. Only 14 of Davis' fit for use. Got my horse shod and waited for a while to see if the man I left behind came in. As there were no signs of him I pulled out about 2:00 A.M. on the following day. Reached camp about 7:30 A.M. having made a ride of about 70 miles in the night. On reaching Pantano I telegraphed General Miles, at Tucson, a report of the situation, and received orders to take the trail and follow it into Mexico or wherever it led as rapidly as possible. While in Davis' camp learned from them that a considerable party of armed ranchers had followed the Indian trail some distance beyond our camp. This accounts for the marks of shod horses on the trail and for its being difficult and hard to follow. To the best of my recollection, the distance made with Finley was 20 miles; distance during the night 65-70 miles.

May 30th, 1886
Left Davis' camp at 2:00 o'clock [sic] this morning, and

had a rather dark and lonesome ride back. Had hard work to follow the trail and covered a good deal of extra ground, possibly 35 miles, perhaps more. Went as near as possible to where the man was left last night, and crossed what seemed to be his trail leading toward Tucson, to the left. Went on to camp, and by hard riding reached there about 7:30 A.M. Rode a good part of the distance at a sharp trot, as the country in places was pretty good. Got some breakfast, turned my horse in to the packtrain, and started out on foot with the Indians. We marched along the West side of the Santa Ritas, making long detours up into the canons looking for signs of the hostiles. Found some freshly killed beef. The country was difficult, and practically no water. Passed water only once during the day, and that was poor in quality and small in amount. Weather intensely hot. At one point, on coming up on a divide, saw what we thought to be Huachuca in the distance.

At length we had to turn down towards the Santa Cruz valley for water, making in all a hard day's march of upwards of 30 miles. Camped on the Santa Cruz near the house of a Yaqui Indian, where Lawton and I got supper, consisting of tortillas, venison, and coffee, at the rate of 50¢ per head. Made my bed up after dark, and found before long that it was on a large anthill. Reached camp about 3 miles ahead of the Infantry, came in with the Indian Scouts. For the last 7 miles we came at a dog trot. I remember distinctly that the last 5 or 6 miles running and walking seemed almost automatic, I was so thoroughly tired.

May 31st, 1886

Resumed trail this morning at daybreak and followed it all day, passing water only once, at the spring Agua Caliente about 20 miles in an air line from Columbia Smelter, our detour last night for water having taken us a long distance from the trail. We picked up the hostiles' trail again and during the day came on one of their camps on a backbone leading up into the Old Baldy Mountain,[38] which is the highest peak in the Santa Ritas. The camp was on the top of a very high peak, and we had a hard

difficult climb up to it. Found it abandoned. Evidences of com-
paratively recent occupation. From here the train turned southwest, and as the Infantry could avoid much hard marching by
cutting across to south we sent back an Indian runner to Territt
with instructions to turn them off. The party which had come
up with us to the Indian camp consisted only of the Indian
Scouts, Lawton, and myself. By this we were able to save the
Infantry several miles of hard marching. The trail led through
the foothills down to the Santa Cruz River, crossing it at a point
about 7 miles west of Calabasas, and struck from there into the
Pajarito Mountains at a point near where they came out on their
raid north.[39]

I went on ahead with the Indian Scouts to look up a camping
place, and found a very decent one near the Tumacacara [sic]
Ranch, named from an old abandoned mission near that point,
built many years ago by the Catholic Missionaries.[40] All about
this mission are signs of irrigation, and evidences that at one
time there was much cultivated land in this region. Walsh,
whom we left at Calabasas when we went north, has been at
Tubac[41] for a few days with a troop. Reports here indicate that
he has returned to Calabasas, passing through about 11:00 A.M.
today. Took a shave and had a delightful bath in the river today.
30 - 32

June 1st, 1886
Moved our command to a camp near Calabasas this
morning, for supplies and refitting. Lt. Noble, 1st Infantry, was
there. I telegraphed to be sent to Huachuca to refit medical supplies necessary for the expedition into Sonora. Some of the
packers quite sick today, in camp. Obtained permission to go in.
Nothing especially new today. Returned to camp after the arrival of the mail. No letters, but a lot of papers.

June 2nd, 1886
Got up at 4:00 A.M., and went up to the railroad. On the

way up stopped at Noble's camp and at the hotel to see what was wanted at Huachuca. On arriving at Huachuca found Colonel Royal[42] and Dr. Brown at the station. The doctor was going to Grant on court-martial duty, and the Colonel to Wil[l]cox to see General Miles. The Colonel gave up his trip. Dined with the Colonel and Miss Royal[43] at Huachuca. Miss Hortense Beaumont also there. Slept at my own quarters. Called on Lt. Johnson, who was under arrest at the hotel, awaiting trail or other action.[44] Received orders to go to [Fort] Grant[45] as a witness before the general Court-martial, case of Lt. Ward,[46] 10th Cavalry, who recently got into trouble at Crittendon, drunk and disorderly.

June 3rd, 1886

Left at 8:30 A.M. for Fort Grant, arriving after a rather tiresome trip. Put up at the hotel on arrival and reported to the Adjutant. Called on Colonel Shafter, met Mrs. and Miss Shafter.

June 4th, 1886

Was at the post all day. Called as a witness in the Ward case. Made some official calls in the afternoon. Finished up the case. Doherty, 1st Infantry, Judge Advocate. Was asked the cause of Ward's sudden case of delirium tremens. Was reluctantly compelled to state that it was caused by the sudden cutting off of his regular supply of liquor after being placed under arrest. Court seemed to consider this as evidence in his favor.

June 5th, 1886

Left Grant early this morning and came to Wil[l]cox. Mr. Norton, Post Trader, came with me. Called on General Miles and had several hours talk with him before the train came in. Dapray, A.D.C., and Thompson,[47] adjutant, both here with the General. Westbound train 13 hours late, so I took dinner and a room at the Arizona House and employed my time writing up the diary. Learned that Lawton has gone into Huachuca to get supplies for refitting. The command is at Calabasas. In the evening I called on Mrs. Stewart, where the General and Dapray are stopping. Train arrived about 9:00 P.M. and I went on to Benson Junction. Put up at the Virginia Hotel until the train left for Huachuca.

June 6th, 1886

Took the train for Huachuca. General Miles, Dapray and Major [A. S.] Kimball are on the train. They are going down to Calabasas. Left the train at Huachuca and went up to the post with General Forsythe, who was at the station to meet the train. Called on General Forsythe,[48] the Royals, Captain Parker, and Lt. [Alexander] Patch.

June 7th, 1886

Very busy this morning, getting supplies ready to ship to Calabasas, and fixing up things at the post. Received a telegram that Lawton was on the trail with outfit, and that I am to go to Calabasas and join him there. Pulled out on the afternoon train, and found on reaching Calabasas that Benson was the only officer left, and that the packtrain was with him. Lawton left this morning and joined Walsh in the Patagonia Mountains, where he, Walsh, had run into an outfit of hostile Indians, captured their stock, etc. Walsh left the camp on Sunday morning and took with him nearly all the troop and 13 Indian Scouts. Finley went out Monday, took 11 men (Cavalry) and 7 Indians.

June 8th, 1886

Supplies have come in. In camp all day. Busy getting things in shape for the final start into Sonora. General Miles is at Calabasas. Had several talks with him during the day.

June 9th, 1886

General Miles and Dapray went to Tucson this morning. Benson and I went to see them off. One man returned from Lawton, sent in on account of sickness. Reports command following

45

hard on trail. Camped at 9:00 P.M. last night. Command is moving with stripped saddles,[49] and following a large plain trail into
Las Pinas Mountains and along their summits. He is said to be
close to the Indians. Pulled out again at 2:00 A.M., no fires
allowed for cooking. Thirty Mexican half-breeds and Yaqui Indians, all a poor lot, came up from Nogales, under a man called
Hank Frost. These men are supposed to be a valuable adjunct
for our force. A more dejected and worthless lot I have never
seen, and it is safe to say that they will be useless. Benson issued
them flour and bacon for the night, refusing to give them anything more, as it is evident they will not be fit for service.[50] No
further news from Lawton.

June 10th, 1886
    In camp all day, nothing of special note. An order came
in from Thompson, A.A.G., to proceed to Ojo de Agua and meet
Lawton. A little later Billy Long, a courier, came in with an
order from Lawton to proceed to the same place with packtrain
and remaining men of Cavalry, and go into camp there. Benson
also ordered to Huachuca in person to attend to some money
matters and arrange further details about supplies. Returned to
camp at 10:00 P.M. and arranged to pull out early in the morning. Very glad to get rid of this Mexican outfit and the delay in
camp.

Part II: *The Chase*

Chapter 2: *Searching for Trails in Sonora Province*

"Somebody must do something and I am going to try to do it. So far we have had no chance. Be nice to Miles for I am working for a reputation and I want his good favor and all the credit I can get from him."

Lawton to Mame, June 21, 1886

"This is godforsaken country and godforsaken people living in it. . . . I really do not feel any sympathy when I hear that the Indians have killed a half a dozen or more of the people. I think the Indians better than the Mexicans."

Lawton to Mame, June 30, 1886

June 11th, 1886

Benson and I left camp at 5:00 A.M., went to the station to get supplies which came down from Huachuca last night and arranged everything for the packtrain, and saw the things packed. Then pulled down the Santa Cruz Valley towards Buena Vista. Benson left me in charge and started across country to Huachuca. I marched down to the Mescatel Ranch, Chatto Martinez' brother's place, and went into camp with the packtrain, which had already arrived there. Purchased 854 pounds of dry alfalfa hay. Have with me 61 animals, 49 mules and 12 horses, not including cavalry escort and packer's mounts.

Chasing Geronimo

June 12th, 1886
Left camp at 5:00 A.M. and marched down the trail by
the Santa Barbara Ranch and then on down the canon to the Ojo
de Agua. Passed the ranch a mile or two and camped near the
Yaqui huts at a point about 1½ miles southeast of the old mission. Bought some dry forage for the stock. Despatches from
Huachuca for Lawton came in, also Fisher who was left sick at
Ojo de Agua. One of the Mexican packers, Joe, came into camp
from Lawton with instructions to put us on Lawton's trail by
cutoff. With him came Vinton (Jerome) and an Indian, who
was on the back trail to get Dolly, Lawton's mule, which had
again gotten away and started back. While things were being
packed up in camp, went ½ mile down creek to ranch belonging
to a man named Manuel Griego, who had a daughter very sick
with malarial fever.

June 13th, 1886
Lying in camp today, waiting for supplies which are en
route from Huachuca. I went out in the morning with a shotgun
and picked up 18 large pigeons in the chaparrel [sic] thickets
near camp. These birds are very good eating, and weigh about
one pound each. The packers are improving the stop to set up
aparejos[1] and make everything ready for the hard trip in the
mountains. About 2:30 P.M. Lt. Territt, 8th Infantry, whom
Lawton relieved at Calabasas in the trip across country from
Pantano because he found him useless for hard field service,[2]
came with 26 packmules and about 3,300 pounds of supplies. He
declined to let me have any additional mules, so I took all I
could in addition to our present loads, amounting to about 2,500
pounds, and sent back the remainder, 1,000 pounds, with a
statement why we had not taken it. Made a very serious effort
to have him transfer some mules, but he was afraid to do it. Also
tried to have him go along with the extra mules until we met
Lawton. This he declined to do, claiming he had received orders

50

from Colonel Royal to return promptly and not to turn anything over in the way of stock.

I sent Vinton and Indians on to Lawton this morning with Dolly, and notified that everything was ready to follow tomorrow. Wrote out a general report showing what clothing and supplies we have for General Miles in accordance with his request, Private Roland acting as clerk. Late in the afternoon old man Streeter, known as the white Apache on account of his long experience with the Apaches and supposed knowledge of and friendship with them, came into camp with orders to report for duty with us.[3] With him came Allsup, who had been sent back to Huachuca for something or other.

June 14th, 1886

Early this morning Territt pulled out for Huachuca and I for Lawton. The Mexican, Joe, acted as our guide and took us up a long backbone. The command left the valley, to the southeast, climbing this big backbone just before entering the canon down which the creek runs to the ranch. The canon which we turned into and from which we climbed up the backbone, is the one just north of the canon in which the stream runs. The trail was pretty fair for a long time, and it looked as though we would get over the Blue Mountains without much trouble, but about noon we struck an immense canon down which we struggled, rolling mules and horses from time to time. Had a difficult time generally. We finally got over and went up a long hill and down another, and camped on a canon leading up to the main final divide which runs up to the peak of the Great Blue Mountains. Had good water, but it is an ugly hole to get caught in by Indians. We only have a few men with us. We gathered up our stuff, secured broken packs, and got something to eat, then packed up and pulled up over the divide. Had a very difficult trail, steep and almost impassable in places.[4] About dark we crossed the main divide. A lot of dead horses on the divide, showing where the Indians had killed broken down stock.

After we crossed the divide we went down in the night, a good moon, one of the most difficult trails I ever saw. Rolled a number of mules, and I never heard worse cursing by packers than occurred this night.[5] The side of the canon in many places as we were going down consisted of rock covered with leaves and pine needles, looking all right until the mules got on it, and then they went shooting down to the bottom. Finally we struck a little water down in the canon near the beginning of the foothills. We went into camp, posted outpost, got our animals out, did what we could in the way of a herd guard, pretty much everybody dead with fatigue. Old Streeter constantly reporting signs of Indians, evidently very much alarmed. Allsup no use, afraid to go out any distance. Billy Long, the Indians and packers did practically all the guard.

Private Noble, B Troop, came back with a note from Lawton, also letter to be sent into Huachuca; sent Billy Long in with it.[6] This man has done excellent work. A good frontiersman, quiet, and entirely fearless. Noble had been left at Lawton's last camp, which is only about 2 miles ahead of us, and the Mexican, Joe, and Long, whom I had sent ahead to see if we were anywhere near Lawton, found him in camp and brought him in. We made camp in this canon about 10:00 P.M.

At 1:30 A.M. Sergeant Cabaniss and Private Eastman, with a lead packmule, came into camp from Lawton, who is about 15 miles away. They brought an order for rations, command entirely out of everything. Gave them flour and bacon and started them back at once. Shortly afterwards the mule returned, minus his pack, and created a stampede in camp, as he came tearing up the trail, stirring up our herd. Finally caught him. Cabaniss and party came back, took the mule to the point where the pack was lost, reloaded, and went back to Lawton's camp. Kept a sharp lookout all night against possible surprise by Indians. We have with us a large amount of money for Lawton's expenses, and about 3,000 extra rounds of ammunition, which would come in handy if taken by the Indians. Marched 25 miles, equal to 60 or 70 miles in ordinary country.

June 15th, 1886

Pulled out at 6:00 A.M. over a very rough trail, about as rough as anything we have had. We ran along the side of a very ugly canon, in places hundreds of feet down. Lost one mule, who went over, making a sheer fall of probably 200 feet. We could look down and see that the body was split open and that the cargo was badly broken up and scattered about. We finally came to a very bad fall off of about 40 feet, down which the mules had to slide, and, in some cases, roll. Fortunately, no animals were killed or seriously hurt, although some of them made a dozen turns in going down.

Came on one of Lawton's old camps about 2:00 P.M. near a place which the maps show to be an old mining district, known as the Santa Teresa, but not worked for many many years. We lay here for an hour and got a bite to eat, then pulled out again. At this little camp we found good water and grass, and the stock all got a bite. Some suspicious horsemen seen in a canon a little later. Found a little later on looking the trail over that they were Indians. Streeter very much excited. Evidently some hostiles who had cut in behind Lawton to see if there is any chance of catching us napping. Marched all evening and until midnight, camped at 12:30 or 1:00 A.M. in a little canon. Trail during the last few hours very rough. We crossed over the summits of the mountains during the early evening and got through fairly well. Country well timbered and seemed to be a good grass country in open places. The trail of Lawton's command was pretty fresh and we could follow it by moonlight by those in advance walking in places. In other places it could be seen from horseback. We passed one very ugly place on the side of the mountain during the night. The surface was smooth rock covered with mold and leaves, the whole thing running down into a gully or pocket. We piled up three mules one on top of the other in about as many seconds. The packers outdid themselves on this occasion; such language one only hears under these conditions and in similar places. Passed one of Lawton's camps during the night. The ride, despite all the hard work, was interesting and much of it very beautiful. Made a distance of 30 miles through a hard country.

June 16th, 1886

Lay in camp until 11:00 A.M. to rest stock, get something to eat and give the animals a chance to graze. Then pulled out and marched over a rough broken country to Lawton's camp. Two packers, Kimball and the Mexican, Antonio, came on the back trail to meet us. They had some difficulty in following their own trail back, so that we were delayed from time to time. A great many deer in this country. Two or three hours after leaving camp we were met by packers Green and Roarer, who took us into Lawton's camp.

Got into camp about 7:00 P.M. Found it in a very rough canon, water extremely difficult, necessary to send the animals over big piles of boulders. It seemed impossible for them to get down to the water, but they managed it somehow. We camped about a mile from Lawton, who was on the best water. After unpacking, managed to get most of the animals up there as they succeeded in getting very little water near us. Could have moved the whole command up there, but there was no room. I found Lawton, Walsh and Finley up on a cliff overlooking the canon in which the command was camped. Everyone hungry and ugly, pretty well used up. 18 miles.

June 17th, 1886

Scouts out all over the mountain looking for trails. Pack-train and cavalry in camp. Lawton down at my camp during the morning. Our scouts saw some hostiles ahead, but they scattered without a fight. Our camp is in the Cacascas Mountains, on the west side. Allsup and I went out deer shooting in the afternoon. Country is swarming with white tailed deer. Got a large one and brought it into camp. Allsup got lost and did not get into camp until 10:00 P.M. and was the most frightened man I have ever seen. Says he heard distant firing. Country swarms with game, quail, turkey, and deer. Very tired, as I packed the deer, it seemed to me, about 5 miles. Was able to bring in only the 2 hind quarters and a fore shoulder. Walked 16 miles.

June 18th, 1886

Pulled out early with the whole command. Scouts in advance under the 1st Sergeant, Dick. Allsup and I were ahead of the command, and about ½ miles behind the Scouts, whom we overtook about noon. Several Indians who had been with the advance came running back much excited and reported Mexican troops close at hand. We were at this time with the main body of the Scouts, which had halted. Sent Dick and his Indians up among the rocks. The canon here divided. Sent Allsup down one branch and I went down the other. As it was reported the Mexicans were coming, it was hoped that one of us would be able to meet them and stop them. Allsup returned almost immediately from the canon in which he was sent, stating that he saw and heard the Mexicans coming up his side. The division of the canon only ran about ¼ of a mile, then reunited and went on. Just then Lawton came up and he and I went down to meet them, but instead of coming up the canon as Allsup reported they were going the other way as fast as they could. It seems that when they saw our advance guard of scouts they thought they were up against the main body of the hostiles, and with a portion of whom they had had a fight the day before, recovering the little Peck child, who happened to be with this portion of the hostile outfit. They killed one Indian woman and wounded a number of Indians, and had 4 men killed. Lawton, Finley and I followed on after the Mexicans as fast as we could, shouting to them, making signs we were friendly, etc. Finally, they took position on a mesa surrounded by a mass of volcanic rock, and lay there as we came up.

They turned out to be about 80 men, and I think everyone who had a gun had it on us as we came up the trail. It was anything but a pleasant situation, as we knew they did not like us and the chances were about even that someone would let fly at us. It was an awful chase down the canon up over a ridge and across another, before we came up to them. We had to lead our horses, which in some places jumped down sheer falls of 5 or 6 feet. We finally established friendly relations with these Mexicans, and sent back word for the command to come up. We then moved down the canon a short distance, and the two forces, Mexicans and Americans, went into camp on opposite sides of the canon. The Mexicans went in and recovered their dead, 4 all together, all of them shot through the head. The squaw was buried. I have somewhere among my Indian things the string of beads she had on, which were taken off by Williams and afterwards given to me.

On counting up the Mexicans we found there were 65 of them. Their story was that they were hunting for the bodies of their dead when our advance body of Scouts came suddenly upon them. They took them for hostiles who were coming back after the squaw's body, and having had all the fight they wanted pulled out. Allsup's story was simply a coward's tale, he had seen nothing. The little Peck child was badly bruised. It seems that when the Mexicans fired their first volley, they wounded the man who was carrying her and killed the horse, so she fell among the rocks and was badly bruised. She was in our camp today and will be sent back to the frontier. We gave her the best things we had in camp to eat. Reported Allsup's cowardice to Lawton, and he was discharged and sent back with the couriers. Sent Jack Wilson in to Huachuca with despatches. He took the back trail. It is a risky piece of business.

June 19th, 1886
    Up early in the morning and by a winding trail marched down to the Saracachi creek, and camped near the ranch of

Valenzuela. Purchased green forage. Lawton and I went up to the old ranch in the afternoon, also Streeter and the Mexican Joe. Hunted a fairly good camp in the field near the ranch. 8 miles today, over a very rough country.

June 20th, 1886

Moved camp today to a position with better wood and water. Secured plenty of forage for the animals which were badly used up. We had a swim in the creek and managed to get our clothing washed. We also sent a Mexican courier over the mountain to a little town where there are a good many fig trees. He made the ride during the night to avoid the Indians and came back in the morning with about 20 pounds of fresh figs. Had the Indians make me a pair of moccasins today to replace those worn out.[7] Finley and Streeter went out on a reconnaissance toward the Sonora River. Went through to Sinoquipe to investigate certain Indian rumors. Had a sufficient escort with them.

June 21st, 1886

Command in camp. Scouts out looking over country searching for trails, investigating reports and trying to locate whereabouts of Indian parties.

June 22nd, 1886

Command still in camp. Lawton received a ridiculous message from the prefect of the District of Montezuma, directing him not to proceed further into the territory of Sonora. No attention paid to it.[8] Billy Long, Tom Horn[9] and 3 soldiers, men of the troop, came into camp today, riding Mexican mules. All their horses were stolen a night or two ago at Pesquera's ranch from a field near the house in which they had put them for the night. Long and Horn, accompanied by a party of Mexicans from the ranch followed the trail but found nothing except abandoned horses.

57

Chasing Geronimo

June 23rd, 1886

Streeter's man returned from Sinoquipe with Finley's report. No definite news of the Indians. Reports indicate fairly good grass and forage in the Sonora River Valley near Sinoquipe. Whole command pulled out, moved up the canon to camp with better water and grazing near the old Mescal ranch. 12 miles

12

Chapter 3: *A Coming Fight*

"The whole country is a mass of gigantic mountains through which we are laboriously working on the trail of the ever fleeing and never fighting Indian."

"We surprised Geronimo today. We made a force march across a mountain in terrible heat. Five men out of twenty fell out. We marched in undershirt, cotton pants and carry only ammunition, rifle and water."
Wood to Mother, July 14, 19, 1886

June 24th, 1886

Command left camp early in the morning and marched across country to Sinoquipe, reaching there about 1:00 P.M. Got some dinner near the San Agustin Mountain. The men went up into town during the night, a good many ugly fights, due to mescal.[1] Lowry badly stabbed, but will live. Walsh out most of the night, looking up men. Distance marched today 25 miles. The trouble here tonight was largely due to the people of the town giving the men all sorts of strong drink.

25

June 25th, 1886

Benson arrived during the day. Came down from Huachuca. Brought in some reports, and the latest news. Command lay in camp. Scouts investigating country and trying to locate trail. Called on the Presidente of the town. We are waiting here for a new allotment of scouts, as the enlistment of our present scouts runs out this month. Also waiting for the detail of infantry which is coming down from Huachuca.

June 26th, 1886

R. A. Brown, 4th Cavalry, came in today with the new scouts and Infantry. Men, generally speaking, in good condition, but infantry in bad condition of discipline. It seems that they have no officer with them. Very badly shod. One or two men not strong enough to go on. Ordered them sent back. The acting 1st Sergeant was brought into camp with his hands tied behind him and his gun lashed across his back. One or two other men have been insubordinate. General condition due to lack of officers and a feeling on the part of the men that they have been neglected and badly treated.[2] Mailed some letters from Sinoquipe, which is a typical Mexican village, with church and adobe houses. These people are civilized Indians, with only a moderate strain of white blood.[3]

June 27th, 1886

Left camp at 7:00 A.M. Indians on ahead. Temperature in the sun about 127 degrees. Marched down the trail to Las Delicias ranch, via the town of Banamachi. Had a good camp but the water was poor at it comes from a hot spring, almost intolerable and undrinkable. Has to be cooled before drinking. Also a great deal of impurity in the water. Called for a moment on the Presidente of the town of Banamachi, which is a large town, walled in places, main street paved, etc. Most of the Infantry still ugly and insubordinate. Had to tie some of them up on the march. Forded the river very frequently during the day. Met a Dr. Blaine, who has been about here since '68, and with him visited the St. Helena mine, where there is a large fine mill in good condition, 60 stamps in good order. Blaine whiled away the rest of the evening with tales of the old days under General Pesquera, his own personal troubles and duels, one of which he fought with the Presidente of Banamachi. Distance marched 16 miles.

16

June 28th, 1886

Left camp very early this morning. Brown and I and the Scouts, 30 of them. The 1st Sergeant is Tony, a San Carlos Apache. We stopped at the mill and filled our canteens, then pulled up into the mountains. Our object is to scout the mountains of this section and see if we can locate the hostiles. Jack Frisbee went with us for a distance and showed us where the Indians had done some killing a day or two before, killed some Mexicans. Here we left him and went on by ourselves, marching until 9:30 P.M. when the moon went under and a heavy tempest came up. Made the best shelter we could under bushes and rocks, but got soaked a dozen times over. No supper or drinking water, only a little rainwater. Had a bottle of vermouth, which Brown and I sampled, but with bad effect, as it nearly choked us. Distance marched 16-20 miles.

16-20

June 29th, 1886

Left camp at daybreak and marched about 3 miles before we found water. We were all badly in need of it. Here we stopped to get something to eat and then went on. Found many small rock tanks full of water. This water had been standing for months as we were at the end of the dry season, and it was almost gelatinous in consistency. The forests were on fire in many places, the Indians having set fire to them. The trail is very difficult to follow. Killed one deer towards evening.

Camped on fair grass and water, which is much needed by our stock. Terrific tempest at night. Lightning appalling. We were drenched throughout the night. As far as we can locate ourselves we are about 10 miles south of the east and west trail between

Cumpas and Sinoquipe. The Indians have been searching the country very carefully today for the hostiles. A good many signs of the hostiles, but the trails are scattered. They evidently passed through this country in small parties of two or three.

June 30th, 1886

Pulled out at 3:30 A.M. as soon as we could see the ground and followed the trail which the Indians located yesterday until 10:00 A.M., then we had our first food of the day. Fresh deer meat and salt. Then went on until we struck the Cumpas trail, and camped just south of it on fair grass and water. The trail is about 2 miles east of large peak seen to the eastward from Sinoquipe, which lies west of us about 20 miles. It was very important to find out whether any Indian news had been received at Sinoquipe since I left there. We have with us now as interpreter and in a way chief of scouts an old Mexican by the name of Jose Maria Alias,[4] who was a prisoner of the Apaches from the time he was an infant until he was about 20 years of age. He speaks Apache better than he does Spanish and knows all these Indians. I explained to him the necessity of getting this information, and had agreed with Brown to take 5 Indians and go into Sinoquipe. When the time came to go the Indians refused to go unless the whole outfit went in. This was out of the question, and as I was rather provoked, I decided to go on alone. Old Jose Maria attempted to dissuade me, and when I insisted on going gave me his spurs and cautioned me to lay up until nightfall in case I saw anything suspicious. He seemed to think my chance of getting through was rather small.

Left camp about 4:00 P.M. and after I had been about an hour on the road, while crossing a mesa, noticed the tracks of 8 men wearing moccasins crossing the trail to the north. As it had rained within an hour and these tracks had been made since the rain it was evident that they were not far distant. To make matters worse, my mule, when she crossed this trail, seemed to smell something and gave a loud yell characteristic of a frightened mule. I had an anxious time of it from then on. I took a strong position in the rocks and waited for a while, to see if the mule's bellowing had been heard. Finally I went on. As I got near Sino-quipe I killed a couple of deer and left them across the trail. It was a foolish thing to do, but the temptation was too strong.

Finally reached Sinoquipe, where I found that a man had been killed nearby an hour or two before, evidently by the very Indians whose tracks I had seen. This was the only Indian news in town. Waited until after dark and started back to camp, reaching there about midnight, nearly breaking my neck over the side of a canon down which my mule and I took an ugly roll in the darkness. The object of the trip was to get fresh information about the Indians. This I got. I was unable to find the deer coming back.[5] Total distance about 40 miles.

40

July 1st, 1886
Pulled out of camp at 5:00 A.M. and went on ahead with Lt. Brown and two or three Indians for about 16 miles. Saw and killed some deer which we left for the packers to pick up. Country green and picturesque, rolling, and covered with old lava formation in places. Pine trees very numerous. The last few miles of the march we rode and came into a large canon with pools of fair water on one of which we camped. Brown and I afterwards went down to another pool and had a swim. Deer thick. Brown sent the Mexican packer, Joe, ahead with his report and a note from me to Lawton. Saw a good many signs of Indians today, but the trail was scattered. Indians have been in this country hunting, or looking for stray cattle. Distance marched 21 miles.

21

July 2nd, 1886
Marched as soon as we could see the ground, and followed the canon down. Much water as we went on. When near

the town [of Cumpas] I went ahead to get permission to march through with the Indians, but the Presidente did not like the idea, so we went around. Found Lawton and Benson in camp about a mile from town, Cumpas. Weather hot, about 120 degrees in the shade, terrifically hot and dry. No especial news in camp concerning the hostiles. Brown made his report. It looks as if the Indians have scattered, to come together at some further point.[6] Old Streeter is still with us. About 100 sick people came out from the town to see me and get some sort of medicine.[7] Infantry still without an officer and greatly in need of some one to take charge of them. I volunteered and was placed in command today. The men are pretty badly demoralized. Lawton agreed, upon my suggestion, to withdraw all charges against the men under arrest. I gave them a plain talking to and told them I would do the best I could with them and for them. Distance marched today 18 miles.

18

July 3rd, 1886

Marched at 4:00 P.M. with the Infantry. We took a rapid gait, a short trot at times, crossing and recrossing the stream many times during the afternoon, and reached camp at a point about 10 miles from Oposura about 9:00 P.M. Near our camping place we found a surveying party under Lt. Flipper. Lt. Flipper was formerly a Lieutenant of the 10th Cavalry.[8] The men marched splendidly and seemed cheerful. Distance made 17 miles.

17

July 4th, 1886

Marched at 5:00 A.M. and got into Oposura [Moctezuma] about 8:00 A.M., passed through the town to camp 4 miles below. Weather simply broiling hot. After packtrain came in Lawton and I went up to the town and had a long talk with the officials. Later on I went down to see the old padre, who is a fine old fellow of Spanish descent, and has been ill for a long time. He lives in a very good house, everything neat, two sisters take care of him. He has with him a very beautiful niece, one of the prettiest girls I have ever seen in this part of the world. Gave the old gentleman an order for some medicine and such good advice as I could. A fine old church here, built of volcanic rock, dates from about 1600. Distance marched today 14 miles. Oposura, or Moctezuma, as it is sometimes called is a rather fine town, situated in a fertile, well watered valley. Some fairly good stores. Everything comes into these towns on the backs of pack-mules and burros. No wagon roads anywhere. The history of the town is one long struggle with hostile Apaches, who have raided this country for the past two or three hundred years.

July 5th, 1886

Went up to town this morning with Captain Lawton. It rained some during the night and the ground was pretty wet and slippery. Operated on a Mexican officer's daughter for strabismus. A rather good case for operation. Lawton helped. Father seemed very grateful.[9] He was the prefect of the district. Mexican troops returned today, confirm reported killing of some people by Apaches. Went up to town again in the afternoon, had a long talk with the prefect and got an order for some guides. Flipper was in town today. Distance ridden, 16 miles.

16

July 6th, 1886

Moved out of camp at 4:15 P.M. and marched 7 miles down toward Tepachi, where we were overtaken by a courier from the prefect with the news of fresh Indian depredations 13 miles due east of Oposura or slightly southeast, so swung to the eastward in a direction to cut the trail which would take us to a mescal ranch where the Indian depredations are reported. Found one wounded Mexican there, shot last night. Cut the bullet out of his shoulder.

We had a terrifically hard march today. The heat was intense. The guide mixed up his leagues with miles and when we swung off to take the trail told us we had only a little over 4 miles to go. The march was the worst I have ever seen. It consisted of pure volcanic rock which covered the ground in a layer anywhere from 3 to 4 to 15 feet deep. Some straggling bushes came up through it in places. Had to finally send the packtrain around by a long detour. The men's shoes were badly torn up and they were about dead when they reached camp. In fact, I was rather worried lest they shot the guide on sight. The water at the spring was so hot that neither men nor animals could drink it, and it had to be taken out and cooled before using. Rain came on shortly after our arrival, and it rained all night, with fearful lightning. No grazing. Plenty of wood. Weather hot and muggy. The men, when we reached camp, were frantic for water, but, as stated, the spring water could not be used until cooled. Our Indians were out shortly after reaching camp and soon located the trail of the Indians who did the shooting. Report that they were three in number. Total distance marched about 19-20 miles.

19 - 20

July 7th, 1886

Pulled out at 5:00 A.M. Marched 5 miles. Country rough, ground sloppy and muddy from last night's rain. Much cactus. Very difficult for Infantry and Indians. Indians located a spring of cold water and recommended that the command halt there until they could go ahead and work out the trail, which was done. They returned about 12:00, reported the trail of two large horses and a mule leading almost south. About 3:00 P.M., Brown, with 15 Indians started out on trail, to follow it as long as possible tonight and tomorrow, and to halt on good water. We were to follow with the balance of the Indians and the rest of the command. The plan is that we are to go on and camp on the first good water, and that he will send back a runner to that point with any news. We are then to go on or remain, as the circumstances indicate. Pouring rain nearly all night, frightfully hot and close. Main command made 8 miles today.

8

July 8th, 1886

Moved out at 5:00 A.M. sharp. Marched due south 4 miles, then swung a little west for two miles, then the trail led into a canon leading southwest. The trail is through rough rolling country with much water from last night's rain, also a reasonable amount of wood and grass. It has been recently burned over in some places. Camped on good water which seems to be permanent. Evidently very little water in this country in the dry season. Our Indians did some wonderful trailing, keeping the trail for miles when it seemed to be all washed out. Found Brown here. No rain in this particular spot. Ten deer killed near camp this afternoon. Everybody cleaning up, fixing up moccasins. Lawton writing his letter home. Brown cleaning his rifle. Marched 10 miles.

10

July 9th, 1886

Marched at 5:00 A.M., trail running southeast by south. Went 10 miles over rough country. Good grass and wood. Went into camp at 10:30 A.M. Indians found and kept the trail but with much difficulty, as it had been badly washed out. Shortly after striking camp Lawton took Privates Huber and Williams, and went to Tepachi. I went with him. This little town is situated in the canon, every house walled and fortified, distance about 11 miles from camp. Here we got a fairly good meal of Carne Seca, peppers, with some fairly fresh figs, also a feed of corn for our horses. We also learned that the people here had seen hostiles the morning before. Got back to camp before dark. Distance marched by command, 10 miles, by Lawton and myself, 32 miles.

10 - 32

Chasing Geronimo

July 10th, 1886

Left camp at 5:00 A.M. and pulled along slowly through a very rough country. No water except a little left from the rain, and hotter than ——. Went into camp on water in a deep tank down in a small canon; had to pull it up in camp kettles for the stock. Shortly after getting into camp Walsh came in with the packtrain and the cavalry. We had with us at this time the scouts and infantry. Horses looking very thin. Walsh is to go back in the morning. A great mistake, his coming out with the troop, as horses should have been left at Oposura at the supply camp to pick up while this work was being done as the country is so rough here that it is impossible to ride and there is little for the horses to do.[10] Drew ten days rations for the Infantry, who are doing excellently well. Brown is on ahead this afternoon with his Indians. 15 miles.

15

July 11th, 1886

Pulled out at 8:00 A.M. Lateness of the start due to issuing of rations, packing new loads, etc. Received $60.00 commissary money and $150.00 Quartermaster's money, which was sent me by Benson, who is at Oposura. Found rations short, and sent word to Benson to that effect. Trail runs south and a little east of south. Camped on what appears to be permanent water on a large plateau on top of the main range. Fine grass and plenty of wood. Tony, the first sergeant of the Scouts, came back to us, reporting Indian Scouts to be on trail which leads over large mountain bounding our camp on the east. Trail said to be fresh. Heavy tempest all about us. Numerous palms struck by lightning. Lightning so heavy that men and animals badly frightened. Lawton and I found shelter under a large boulder. Put our rifles far distant from us. A number of trees set on fire despite the rain. Am suffering much from a tarantula bite which I must have gotten last night. Walsh went back to Oposura today. Trail exceed-

ingly rough. Distance marched today 10 miles.
10

July 12th, 1886

Left camp at 5:30 A.M. and marched south for 6 miles through a very rough country, when we came to a sudden jump off in the foot of the canon down which we marched. This was about 15 feet deep, and we had to climb around and get our animals over an awfully rough trail. Mules and horses slid and tumbled. Once down we found a fairly good trail leading down the canon toward the Yaqui River. We came to the river and crossed to the other side. Found a dense thicket of cane through which we forced our way, following the trail made by the hostiles. Many animals cut by the sharp cane leaves. These wounds will give us no end of trouble, as this country swarms with blow-flies, and every precaution has to be taken to save our animals. On crossing the river we learned that Brown and the Indians were camped about 1 mile up the stream, most of the way through cane brake. We again crossed the river again and found a camping place on low rocky ground near the river. All hands took a swim, or rather a bath, water low greenish in the pools. Rocks and sand so hot it was impossible to pass over them with bare feet. Had to leave our clothes where the rocks were well shaded.

I am suffering very much from the effects of the spider bite, which has left the parts affected swollen so much that I have had to lance them in places to avoid pressure. Body badly chafed. Brown, with the Scouts and 2 days' rations, pulled out at 2:30 to look up the trail. Private Reynolds gave out today, and I had to have him brought into camp on Brown's mule, which is with the packs. Distance 10 miles, but equal to 30 in ordinary country.
10

July 13th, 1886

Left camp at 5:30 A.M. and marched up the river, winding our way along the sides of the canon, and then back over the hills and mountains. In fact, anywhere that a passable trail could be found. After 5 miles of this we came to a place where Brown camped last night, and at this point the trail swung into a canon which branches off to the left of the river, a lofty range separating the two, that is, the river and the canon. After about 5 miles of this canon we met an Indian courier with word from Brown that his Scouts had located the hostile Chirachua camp, and asking us to let out and come with all speed, which we did, double quicking much of the way. This P.M. 20 men fell out after about 8 miles of this work.

We then came to a place where the trail left the canon to the right and struck over the big mountain towards the river, on which the river, the Indian courier said, the hostile camp was located. Lawton, up to this time, had been riding, and was naturally impatient at what seemed to him the slow gait of us who were on foot. Here we opened our ammunition boxes, filled the [cartridge] belts and had the men put some in their pockets. The heat was so great that it was impossible to handle chisels or anything of steel to open boxes, so opened them by dropping them on sharp pieces of rock and breaking the covers. Heat terrific. Stones so hot they could not be held in the hand where they had been exposed to the full rays of the sun. We then started up the trail, canteens full, everything that made a noise tied up. Captain Lawton soon became almost exhausted from overheating as he had set a very rapid pace and had drank freely of water just before starting. However, with characteristic pluck, he pulled himself together and we all went on. We had only gone a short distance when he turned to me and said: "I now realize that you people have been marching hard all day." In fact, we were up with him all this time, in spite of the fact that we had been on foot all the morning. We were on the sunny and lee side of the mountain, so there was not a breath of air. This climb was the hottest I ever made.

On reaching the summit we could see by looking through a crack in an outlying ledge the Indian camp far below us on the Yaqui. It was situated on a little ledge or plateau, hemmed in on two sides by mountains, which seemed to come down to the river above and below the camp. We were on the Indian trail into the camp, which was plainly marked before us. Fires were burning, Indian ponies picketed out, a good many Indians, men, women and children, moving about in all directions. Looking down from above there seemed to be no outlet, but we knew there must be a good one or the Indians would not be there, as they would be the last to put themselves in a trap.

As soon as the command was assembled Brown was directed to take the Indians and make a flank march to the left, keeping carefully under the ridge and under cover, and to come down to the river well above the camp. Lawton was to remain with the balance of the command, which consisted of the Infantry, the packers having been left in the canon at a place where they could defend themselves. We were pretty well satisfied that the Indians could not get out below and felt that if we waited until Brown was in position we could then commence our advance and work down and force them into Brown's hands as they tried to escape up the river. We felt that the fight would be a pretty ugly one, as the country was extremely rough and there was abundant shelter for the Indians. The Infantrymen who had played out and were unable to get over the ridge we left with the packtrain as an additional protection for it. We all felt very much excited as we had apparently in our hands the people we had followed so long and so hard. After the necessary time had passed we commenced to work our way down towards the camp, keeping in open order and out of sight, utilizing the cover as well as we possibly could. Lawton had one end of the Infantry line and I the other.

About this time heavy firing began on the up river side. We then advanced pretty rapidly and finally were in the bottom land near the camp, and were then fired into by a body of our own Scouts (Brown's Scouts) who were advancing toward us, having found no Indians in the camp. The volley was accidentally sent in our direction. We captured everything in the camp except the

71

Indians, who had been warned by one of their number, who had been out hunting, as we afterwards learned, and had crossed the trail of our Scouts, crossing behind them as he came into camp. He had scrambled and slid down the rocks into camp and got there in time to give the warning. The hostiles, realizing their danger, abandoned everything except their arms and dashed up the narrow trail between the river and the cliff, going up the stream, and must have gotten through just before Brown closed the outlet. It is a wonder that some of us were not killed in this affair. Brown fired several shots at the Indian Chicken, his own striker, taking him for a hostile. Chicken finally protested in very profane English, and Brown turned his attention to other things.

On reaching camp I realized for the first time how sick I had been. Wound tremendously swollen, had to lance it repeatedly. A good deal of pain. Our packtrain was not up and there was no prospect of its getting in before morning or late at night, so I found a quiet place where the water was fairly still near the river bank, sat down with the water up to my armpits and remained there most of the night. This rather eased things up. It took the weight off and took a certain amount of fever out. About midnight the packs came in. We got blankets, and I secured some medicine. Lawton badly used up from exhaustion. Everyone bitterly disappointed over the loss of the Indians and unable to account for their getting the alarm. (The note herein inserted about the way they did get the information came to us later on, when we were taking them in as prisoners of war.)

Marched today 24 miles. I believe these 24 miles were equal to 50 or 60 miles in ordinary country. We were all, with the exception of myself, in good shape and stimulated by the excitement of a coming fight, and did not realize how completely exhausted we were until the whole thing was over. The infantrymen who had played out on the road came in with the packs. Nothing serious, but they were pretty well worn out.[11]

24

Chapter 4: *The Depths of Despair*

"Lawton surprised the Indians on July 14. While their results have not been decisive, yet it has given encouragement to the troops. . . ."

Miles to Drum, July 22, 1886

"I was so disappointed as to be almost sick, for here was the opportunity we had been looking for for so long and it slipped from me. . . . I could cry, Mame, if it would do any good. . . . I hoped I could finish the war and come home but now no one can tell how much longer it will take."

Lawton to Mame, July 14, 1886

July 14th, 1886

In camp all day. Indians out looking up trail, which crosses the river at a trail some miles above. Kept in the water a good deal of the time, during the day, as it eases the pain. In the afternoon felt well enough to try the fishing from where I sat, but got none. The men got a good many catfish which they are eating greedily. A welcome change of diet. Our bacon, which has been carried for long distances in the packs in intense heat, has sweated so much that there is nothing left except the rind and the streaks of lean. The Indians have been very hard at work all day today, and covered a great deal of territory. No white man out with them.

July 15th, 1886

Pulled out at 2:30 P.M. and marched up the river. Trail very rough and difficult, especially near where we left camp. Camped about 5 miles up the river. Came down with severe chills and fever, evidently due to the bite. Parts still dreadfully swollen. The men got many catfish. Marching today caused the greatest pain and discomfort. Trail very difficult and ran between the river and the cliffs, over rock and shifting boulders and shale. No animals lost. Distance made by main command 5 miles.

5

July 16th, 1886

Started out from camp at 5:30 A.M., and after marching about 5 miles over a very rough country I had to take to my horse. Up to this time I had been in the lead with the packs. Was so sick and dizzy that I kept falling down while on foot. Camped after a mile more in a fairly pleasant camp on top of a small divide. Was taken very sick, not expected to live. Delirious all night, with a high fever. Lawton gave me two doses at short intervals of 30 grains of quinine, 60 grain all told.[1] Condition such that he had travois made to send me to Sahuaripa. Heavy rain during the night. I remember the grateful feeling of the cold rain. No shelter whatever. Plenty of grass and water at this camp.

July 17th, 1886

Lay in camp all day. Indians hunting trail, which is very difficult to follow in this country. My fever broke early this morning, and am feeling better, but still very weak. The swelling is commencing to go down. Ground so hot one could hardly sit on it. Brown was very kind to me during the day. Kept my head bound in wet cloths, which, although the water was warm, were damp enough to make it welcome.

July 18th, 1886

The fever left me last night, and I went on today on one

of Lawton's mules, and made the trip without much trouble. Camped on the Arras [sic] River,[2] about 200 yards from the stream. Many deer seen everywhere. Regular fusillade about camp. A rather amusing incident occurred: two deer dashed down through camp to the river. Lawton had gone down to the river to bath [sic]. The temptation was too great, and everyone fired at the deer. On each side of us were high cliffs, and the echoes made it sound as though there were hundreds of shots. Lawton could not tell from the echoes where the shots were coming from and came dashing up into camp as naked as when he was born, with his clothes under his arm. Pretty much everywhere were what we call "Baby Cactus," which stuck up only half an inch above the ground. He filled his feet with this and when he reached us he was ripping mad. His language will not bear repeating. As he lay on a blanket, still cursing, I, assisted by others, tried to get the cactus burrs out of his feet, which we finally succeeded in doing. It was very painful for him, but extremely ridiculous. Brown and one or two Indians helped in getting the stickers out of his feet. Plenty of deer meat in camp.

July 19th, 1886

Pulled out of camp about 5:30 and marched along the [Arros] river for about a mile, and over it to the north side. Cut in over some foothills in order to get a better trail and finally came back to the river, which we forded, then marched about 3 miles further along a very rough trail along the river bank, through heavy sand which was very hard for those on foot, and finally struck the Nacori-Sahuaripa trail. Found that the Indians had gone out on it for a short distance. Followed and camped about four miles from the river. Indian Scouts have done very little work during the last few days, as they have been driving along a lot of worthless horses captured in the hostile camp, and as a result many of them have been behind the Infantry. The trail for the last few days has been very rough and one has to go with the greatest caution or the whole thing gets cut up. Taken as a whole, it is an extremely rough bad country. Many deer. Tremendous amount of cactus of all varieties.

14

July 20th, 1886

The trail at this point is indistinct. It is evident that the Indians have to strike out to get a new mount. Captain Lawton decided that it would be wise to go into Sahuaripa and see if we could possibly get hold of any news, thinking thereby he might be able to strike out for the last place where the Indians were seen and take up a fresh trail there, so he and I, accompanied by three soldiers, Sergeant Cabannis, Privates Williams and Huber, Packers Brown and Coleman, started in to Sahuaripa. We gathered from the very defective map which we had that it could not be more than 20 miles away.

After making 15 miles we came to a quaint old fortified ranch, with a thick high wall of volcanic rock all about the house; the house was built against the wall; inside in the center was a little citadel. About 50 people living here. The whole thing was patriarchal to a degree. One might have been back 2,000 years. The blankets and clothes were pretty much all made from the wool of their own sheep. The women were bringing water from the stream in great big jars which they carried on their heads. Corn was being ground between two flat stones turned by a donkey. In fact, everything was very primitive. This is one of the most remote of the cattle and sheep ranches on the west slope of the Sierra Madre, and the people live here during the greater portion of the year. The place is walled to prevent sudden attack by the Indians. The entrance is only wide enough for one animal to pass at a time. They had a number of arms, but all of them were of a very old type. We met here a man who had just come in from Sahuaripa, who told us it was a good 20 miles further, but we found it a good 30 before we got in. There are fairly good trails between the ranch and Sahuaripa, but it was all up and down hill, and in one place it passed through a great canon where it went along the bottom for 6 or 7 miles, going up and down over great boulders.

Finally, just before dark, we came in sight of the town from the top of a small mountain, and a lovely sight it was to us. The valley was several miles wide, and in the center was the town, with its houses, some of earth colored adobe, others whitewashed and built of stone. A small stream runs through the town, and all about it are fields of corn. There are no wagon roads in this part of the country. In the town is just one wagon, the property of the priest. It was brought up from Guaymas on mules and is never used. Entering the town, we went at once to the house of a Dr. William McClurg Pickett, an old Confederate army Surgeon, and one of the unreconcilables.[3] He has never placed his foot on United States soil since he got over the border after the [Civil] war. He went abroad for a time, and served as a surgeon in the Turkish army during the Russo-Turkish War. He is now very poor and living from hand to mouth. He has an old shotgun, and as pigeons swarm in and about the town he gets most of his meat by potting into a flock of these birds from time to time. He got us a fine large melon and took us over to see the Prefect, who afterwards called on us. The Doctor, in addition to other things, has a small harem, apparently, if we could judge from the number of women about his establishment. Town fairly clean. About 1500 people live here.

45

July 21st, 1886

Up at 5:00 A.M., and after breakfast went to call on the Padre, but found him off on some church work. Afterwards we caught him and had a long talk with him. Found him exceedingly good natured, but rather stupid. He promised to do all he could for us in the way of getting all we wanted in the town and country. He was very proud of two things; one was his church, which was very old and picturesque, and a very quaint and curious set of glass with gold rims which had been in the church for many

many years. Some of this he brought out for us filled with very good mescal. He was, on the whole, a kindly well meaning man. It is wonderful that in this remote country he has retained as much energy as he has. On returning to our camp, or house we found the Prefect there, and Lawton had a long talk with him, while I chatted with the old Doctor. About 11:00 A.M. we left town and marched to the walled ranch which I mentioned above, where we spent the night.

Had a rather rough time getting through the canon. It was dark and all one could do was to tie up the reins and give the mule or horse his head. The animals seemed to realize the danger and went over the trail with their noses to the ground, apparently watching their steps. Before turning in we heard many curious and interesting tales of the Apaches from the Old master of the ranch, tales of Apache raids and doings covering many years. Our animals were fed with small hard corn, which we soaked and softened. Cabannis' horse got hold of some that had not been softened and died during the night of colic. Some of the others also were sick.

30

July 22nd, 1886

Pulled out at 5:30 A.M., Cabannis on foot, and marched for camp. Found the command in camp six miles nearer the ranch than when we left. They had come down to the river, crossed, and camped two miles further on. Two Mexicans came with us for about ten miles. Spent some time after reaching camp in writing some letters, as we shall soon have a courier going in. It rained all night. Also rained last night and the night before. While in the town we got no definite news of the Indians. Whole country very much excited by news of depredations in the west section. No definite news. This country is exceedingly wild and the towns are widely separated. It is 60 miles nearly from Nacori to Sahuaripa, and in all the distance between there is only the one fortified ranch referred to. The men pass through the coun-

try only in armed parties and at rather infrequent intervals.[4]
10

July 23rd, 1886
In camp until 2:00 P.M., when we pulled out and started
for the river. I went on with the Infantry in front of the packtrain. We had a very heavy tempest today. Passed an exceedingly
nasty piece of trail, sloping rock, wet and slippery, with a fall off
of nearly 100 feet. No animals lost in getting over it fortunately.
Much lightning today. Air full of electricity. For the first time
in my life saw indistinct blue balls at the ends of the men's rifles.
Ruined a new pair of Mexican tayuas. Reached camp wet
through. Blankets also soaked. Ground saturated with water. We
are having much trouble with our animals to protect them against
blowflies. These flies lay their eggs in any piece of moist meat and
in a few hours the little screw worms appear which bury themselves in the wound, rapidly multiply and soon destroy the animal. Calomel[5] keeps them out of the wound. Our damp blankets
were full of blowflies today.
12

July 24th, 1886
Marched at 6:00 A.M., forded the river and proceeded up
the Nacori trail 15 miles, camping at a delightful camp on Nacori
Creek, fair shade, etc. About 8 miles of our march were in the
bed of the Creek, constantly crossing and recrossing it, and as
the water was rushing along like a mill race and was up to our
arms, the march was a very hard one on all hands, especially
the Infantry, and we were all tired on reaching camp about 2:00
P.M. We found at the camp the Mexicans we had sent out from
Geronimo's camp on Yaqui river as couriers; they brought word
to us that Torres, the Prefect of the District, had been killed by
some outlaws, and also that no mail had arrived from the United
States. The men were scattered a good deal during the last 2
miles. Killed a beef today, apparently running wild. Took the

brand. A number of wild cattle in this section. Country rolling all about camp.

17

July 25th, 1886
Indians out looking for trail in all directions. Packtrain and Infantry in camp. Everybody glad to halt for a day or two. Many deer in the country. Weather very hot. Heavy rains at night. They are really cloudbursts. Ground is flooded in a few moments. Many mosquitoes and sand flies. Built our bunks well off the ground. Went out shooting, walked 4 miles.

4

July 26th, 1886
Weather very hot and muggy. Went out with 4 men and killed a wild beef after quite a hunt. Took the brand. We have cut out these brands and will take them into Nacori, as this is the only town in this section, and the owners can be paid for them. The cattle here are worth $10.00 gold each, at least that is what they will want for them. The river rose a foot last night. Ammunition was issued to Indians, packers and others to fill up belts today. Distance marched in shooting 7 miles.

7

July 27th, 1886
Command in camp, Indians still hunting for the trail. No definite results. Long reconnaissances being made in all directions. Brown went out with Indians today on trip over the main divide to the east to look for trails, and returned. Hard rains, everything soaked.

July 28th, 1886
Rained in torrents all night. Ground like a lake; our mantas[6] did not make good covers. There are no tents along. Lawton, Cabannis, Huber and a packer, Brown, went up to Nacori

this morning to meet the packtrain we are waiting for. Gave Lawton $10.00 for forage. Busy writing letters, etc. Lawton returned about 2:00 P.M. with the information that packtrain and B Troop from Oposura will be in tomorrow.

July 29th, 1886

Packtrain and troop arrived. Smith and Walsh[7] came out with them. The medicines which I sent for came all right. Walsh has a bad foot and is not in condition to do any work. Smith is full of pluck and energy, rather pulled down, but fit for work.

July 30th, 1886

We sent back the Infantry today. They have done excellent work and done it cheerfully, marching with the Scouts and getting over the ground rapidly. Recommended that Private Harry Graham, D, 8th Infantry, be sent in on account of varicose veins. Also Marshall Hoffman, K, for weak knees; Reynolds, L, for inflammation of the knee; John Maguire, K, with malaria. These men go back to Oposura where they will remain to recuperate. The Cavalry in the meantime take their place for a time. The Infantry and packtrain left en route for Oposura, which is about 75 miles distant, this afternoon. They will make about 11 miles today. The men were in good spirits. Very sorry to see them leave. Was able to give them a fresh issue of shoes and some overalls before they started. These supplies came out on the packtrain. The Cavalry horses show the hard work and although they have picked up in the last few weeks are not yet in good shape. Had a pair of shoes made for Graham with rawhide soles and American leather tops.

July 31st, 1886

A clear morning. Brown and the Indians returned about 11:00 A.M. No signs of hostiles. Out shooting during the morning. Saw many deer but got none, although I had two or three long shots. All downhill shooting and I probably fired high. Brown reports goods scouting country to the east and plenty of water and grass. All hands, except Walsh, took a swim in the small pool near camp. A frightful tempest in the afternoon. Tramped about 7 miles.

7

The work throughout the month has been very hard indeed, and even while the main column has been in camp the Indians and officers have been out scouting the country in all directions. The weather has been hot all day and frightful downpours of rain at night. Country rough. Much of it covered with cactus and not much grass. No men except those in the very best condition could have stood the work. Our food has been poor. Bacon has wasted from the heat until little more than the hide is left. Deer meat has helped us out, with an occasional wild beef from time to time.

August 1st, 1886

Moved our camp this morning to a point on the Nacori Creek, about 3½ miles from the Arras River. Marched down to camp through the bed of the stream. Water quite deep most of the way. Our camp is on rolling hills near the creek, and we have an ample supply of grass, wood and water. Plenty of deer in this section and they are very tame, permitting one to come quite near. Lieutenant Brown and one or two others went down to the Arras to look for the trail of a couple of horsemen reported by Jack Wilson and Edwaddy, and found a plain trail going down to the water's edge. Water so high and river so swift that they did not dare to attempt to cross.[8] Weather exceedingly hot, regular afternoon showers, which are veritable downpours. Thousands of small flies cause much annoyance. The Indians are all out in different directions looking for trail.

15

August 2nd, 1886

This morning Captain Lawton, Brown, Tom Horn and I

went down to the Arras. We found the river very high and running with great swiftness, only the tops of the willows along the bank being out of the water. Current like a mill race and full of drift. Stream about 125 yards wide. Some of the Indian Scouts came down with us to look up the trail, but they would not attempt to cross the river, making signs that they would be pulled under by the current.

Lawton, Horn and I stripped off to try it; a few strokes convinced Lawton that he was entirely out of practice in swimming and that he could not make it. I tried it, followed by Horn, who, when I asked him if he was going on, answered yes, that he did not propose to see me go down alone. I was in good condition for swimming and did not attempt to buck the current, but swam straight across. Was taken down a long distance; an exceedingly hard swim. Horn came very near going under, as although a big strong chap he had not done much swimming in rough water.

No signs of the trail were found on the other side, and whoever the two or three horsemen were they must have been lost in trying to cross the stream, for there were no signs for two or three miles down the stream of their reaching the opposite bank. After a time Brown and some of the Indians crossed the stream higher up, using some logs, etc., as an additional safety. Went well up the stream and swam back, and then went to camp, a distance of 12 miles. The only ugly feature of this stream was its unknown character and the fact that we knew there were rapids not far below where we were trying to cross.

Leonard Wood in Arizona, 1886. The photograph probably was taken just before the long march into Mexico. (National Archives)

Fort Huachuca, Arizona Territory, as it appeared when Leonard Wood was there in 1886. Officers' quarters at left, barracks in center distance, headquarters and stables at right. Huachuca began in 1877 as a camp, was made a fort in 1882, and has been active in recent years. (National Archives)

(*Opposite page*) Noted artist Frederic Remington was in Arizona in 1886 and painted this illustration of Lawton's column for General Nelson Miles' book, *Personal Recollections*. Although not on the expedition, Remington faithfully portrayed the men, animals, and terrain.

Frederic Remington

Leonard Wood appears at far right in this photograph of a search party sent out to seek lost stock after the Lawton expedition returned. (National Archives)

(*Opposite page*) Apache captives photographed at a rest stop while en route east on the Southern Pacific in 1886. Front row (L to R): Fatty, Perico, Naiche, Geronimo, Chapo, and Geronimo's wife. (National Archives)

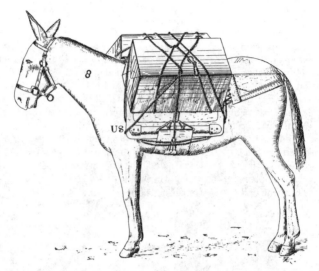

Pack mule loaded with mess boxes, from an Army technical manual written by Lawton in 1882. Few loads were so beautifully symmetrical.

Remington sketched this packer hitching up a cinch in Arizona, 1886. A mule wore a blinder while being packed. The average load was 200 to 250 lbs., according to the animal's own weight.

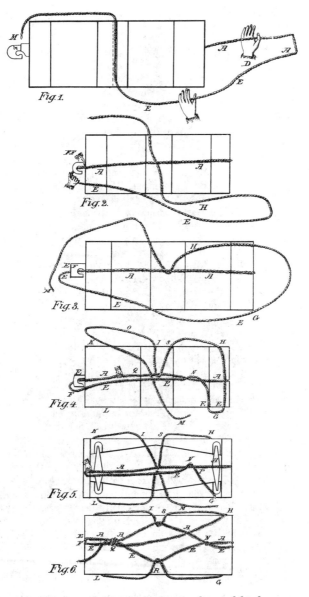

Official diagram for tieing the famous diamond hitch on a mule pack, from the Army manual written by Lawton in 1882.

Geronimo photographed near the Mexican border early in 1886; probably one of several pictures by the Tombstone photographer, C. S. Fly. (National Archives)

Part III: *The Surrender*

Chapter 5: A New Policy

"Gatewood is coming out. He wants me to wait and ask Geronimo to surrender. I shall not wait if I find a trail."

"I will do all I can for Gatewood by making it hot for Geronimo."

Lawton to Mame, August 1, 2, 1886

August 3rd, 1886

Moved camp down to the river to a point just behind the old stone corral on the Nacori-Sahuaripa trail, about 150 yards from the river. As soon as we were in camp I took some men from the train and some enlisted men, and under Captain Lawton's orders went down to the river and commenced getting a ferry rope across so we could raft across our stuff. The river was not quite as swift as yesterday. Swam over, towing a light line. One or two men followed, and we pulled the heavy cable across, which was made of lash ropes twisted together.

While I was doing this A. L. Smith was constructing a raft. The first one was built, apparently of palm logs, which were so heavy that the whole thing sank. Then his party got together a lot of driftwood and made a raft with good flotation. This was covered over with reeds and cane. Smith came down the river on it at a great rate. Inadvertently he stepped just over the edge, which was concealed by the projecting cane and grass, and shot down into the water below. The raft was caught by the rope and served us a good turn in getting things across. Smith, aside from a ducking, was not hurt. As he went through the edge of the raft his big wide hat remained, caught by the branches as he shot down.[1]

During the day James Parker, 1st Lieutenant, 4th Cavalry, turned up.[2] He is camped near our camp of a few days ago. He is escorting Lieutenant [Charles] Gatewood, 6th Cavalry, who has with him two Chiracahua Indians, acting under instructions to send those Indians into the hostile camp at the first opportunity and open up communications with them with a view to their surrender. Gatewood had a long talk with Lawton, and as a result of their conference formally reported to Lawton for duty.

His report was made in writing.[3] The two Apaches he has with him are of the same band which is out, and are among those who remained on the reservation. The instructions which Gatewood has been directed to send to the hostiles are to the effect that they will be followed relentlessly until they are captured, if it takes an age, and that their best chance of receiving clemency is to surrender. Once we are on a fresh trail the plan is to send these Indians on ahead and have them enter the hostile camp and assure them that they will be given safe conduct to General Miles, that they will be protected from the attacks of Mexicans and others while in route. Gatewood stated that he has no faith in this plan and is disgusted with it. Wants to go home. He is not in especially good health. Is suffering from an old inflammation of the bladder which renders riding difficult.[4]

In the afternoon I took 25 Indians and Tom Horn, and started out on a five days' trip.[5] We crossed our things over the river on the raft and swam over ourselves. Our horses and mules also had to swim over. One small Indian by the name of Chicken who could not swim we sent over on the raft. The only saddle animals taken over were two. These were for the two couriers, Lang and Edwaddy, who are going with us for a day and then swing off to cover a lot of country to the south and west. We took no rations except a little coffee and salt; each man carried two belts of ammunition, and an extra pair of mocassins. No blankets or bedding taken. Everyone of our party on foot. We got everything over and started out about 4:00 P.M. I was pretty tired from the hard exercise in the water in the morning and afternoon. We marched 7 miles and camped among some bunches of bushes and grass high up in the mountains. Had some cactus fruit and crackers, which we brought along for the first feed. No fires built. It rained hard during the night. 7 miles today, plus several hours work in the river.

7

August 4th, 1886

Left camp long before light and marched until 9:00 A.M., when we got down into a canon, where we built a fire and made a little coffee and had some freshly killed deer meat. We had only one tin cup for four of us. After about an hour we pulled out and marched until we reached a fortified ranch known as Tepachi Ranch. Here I purchased for $15.00, American money (an exorbitant price) the largest and fattest steer which could be gotten hold of. It was at once shot and cut up, and we all sat around small fires roasting beef in small chunks on our ramrods or on small sticks until well into the night. About 15 feet above the bed of the stream [Nacori Creek] was a cave in the rocks, into which we all climbed, each one getting some straw or branches, or bush, to make a bed. There was just about room for us all to climb in.

During the night we had a very heavy rain, which amounted, in this section, to a cloud burst. The stream rose to the level of the cave and for a time it looked as though it was all up with us as the stream was rushing by with a roar which made conversation difficult. The force of the current was such that the roar of boulders and stones moving in the torrent was distinctly audible. The people in the ranch were very much frightened. There are about 90 people all together; up here for the purpose of making cheese, getting the hides from certain cattle, jerking beef, etc. They have not been out of sight of the buildings for weeks. Dis-

tance marched today, 21 miles, most of it very hard country.
21

August 5th, 1886

Up before daylight and cooked a good deal more fresh beef, and were on the march by daybreak. Edwaddy and Long left us here, with orders to swing down to the south and west by the way of Ures and learn, if possible, if there is any news of the hostiles having been seen in that section. Our object is to cut the Sierra Madre Range from west to east and see if the hostiles have swung north along the divide. Today we crossed some large mountains, all the time headed east. Country fairly good for footmen. Much of our trail running along the backbone of ridges leading up to the high mountains. Late in the afternoon we ran into another fortified ranch, with a stone tower in the center, and a high stone wall all about.

I voluntarily went up ahead to open communications, forgetting that we were a tough looking lot, dressed only in drawers and undershirts, with a ragged handkerchief and the remains of an old campaign hat, and mocassins instead of shoes. The people in the fields all took us for Indians, and ran, shouting, to the ranch: "Los Apaches! Los Apaches." I tried to shout out to them that we were friends, but was answered by a shot which came dangerously near. After a time I managed to convince them that I was not an Indian, and they permitted me to come up to the ranch alone; here, after a good deal of palavering I managed to make them understand who we were and what our objct was. We stopped here for an hour or so, roasting some fresh corn which they gave us, and ate the remaining portion of our meat. We kept the Indians well separated from the Mexicans, they taking care not to come anywhere near our camp. This is a rolling country, good grass and water, elevation about 5,000 feet, I should think.

From here we struck into the heart of the Sierra Madre, crossing some very rough country until we came to the head of a great canon running down to the Arras [sic] River; into this canon we went and after marching until dark camped in it and ate up what little bit of our meat was left over from lunch. We ate all of this steer, nothing was wasted. The Indians ate the entrails, brains, and marrow of the bones, and we carried on with us only the clean solid meat. This great canon which we are now in is fully 3,000 feet deep, and there are only a few places where one can get into or out of it. It is evidently the place where the Arras River comes through the main divide. Where we came down into the canon was risky climbing, and in many places a slip meant a broken neck. No signs of the Broncos.[6] Distance marched 22 miles, but equal to double this distance in ordinary country.

22

August 6th, 1886

Pulled out of camp at daybreak and marched down the canon for eight miles, on what seemed to be an old Indian trail, frequently crossing and re-crossing the small stream in the bottom of the canon. The morning was rather hot and sultry even for this section, and the mountains on each side are covered with a heavy growth of bushes and cactus, and so steep it seems almost impossible to get out.

We finally pulled out of the canon to the left and after two hours of the hardest kind of climbing we reached the top very much scattered and tired. The heat was intense during the climb and the air practically quiet. It was the hardest climb I have had this summer. I went up over the main divide followed by the 1st sergeant of the Indians and nearly all the other Indians. Having gone as far as we thought it wise and as far as we thought there was any reason to believe the hostiles would have gone in going north, we struck straight across the mountains for our camp, which we could see as a white speck on the banks of the Arras River, 25 or 30 miles away. The white speck turned out to be the reflection of the sun on some pieces of canvas which were thrown over some bushes as a shelter. Horn took some of the Indians and bore rather to the right and attempted to reach camp by crossing the country near the river, but did not make nearly as good time as my party, and reached camp 3 hours after we got in. He reported striking a series of box canons which he had to head. The country which we passed over was frightfully rough, but as we were on the main divide we got on all right.

About noon we killed a deer and the Indians made a fire with dry sticks, the first time I have ever seen it done. We killed and ate our deer within an hour of the time he was killed. The singular feature of this hard work in this high and almost impassable country is the intense craving for meat, and the immense amount everyone eats. Nothing takes its place and no ill effects are noticed. I was the third man of our party to reach the river bank opposite camp, sent my gun over on a small raft and swam the stream. Of the 25 Indians on the trip 7 were laid up and all were more or less done up.

25

August 7th, 1886

Lay in camp all day, resting from our hard tramp. Two Indians did not get in until this morning, and a number of them are badly done up. The water in the river is slowly falling, and we will be able to get our horses and packs across soon. Gatewood with his two Indians still with us. He says however, that he wants to go back to Bowie; seems to have no faith in his work. He has approached me in regard to his being sent in on sick report, but I do not think his case warrants it.[7] Millions of small gnats make life a burden here. Near our camp is a strong high old stone corral evidently used as a fortification by the Mexicans in passing through this country, furnishing, as it does, a secure place to camp near water while making the journey from Sahuaripa to Nacori.

Jim Parker and his command started back toward the north today. Since I have been out on this trip he has been camped about 5 miles above here. Lieutenants Richardson, Bullard[8] and Dr. Bannister are with him. Got off some letters today. During our trip we saw no signs of the hostile trail, but it would have been difficult to find it in any case, as the terrific rains which we have had would have washed out the trail of anything except a very large command. It is quite possible that after being put on foot on the Yaqui River the Indians have struck south or even hurried over into Chihuahua.

August 8th, 1886

Two couriers left for the United States and for Huachuca today. Wilson used an old chap by the name of Texas. I sent off my letters by them. Forded the river on my horse today, and found the water deep and swift. Had to raft the plunder over. Just after we had crossed the river we met Long and Edwaddy returning from Sahuaripa and beyond with the news that the Indians had done some killing near Ures and then struck north. This killing was done in the holding up of a large Mexican packtrain, from which they took as many mules as they wanted and a large amount of supplies, flour, canned stuff, etc., which was en route to some of the mines. We marched on to the canon where we camped before, and went into camp. Heavy rain all night.

August 9th, 1886

Lay in camp all day. Close and very hot. Rained exceedingly hard in the evening. Blankets very hard and full of blow flies. Several animals suffering from these pests. Bacon and flour in very bad condition and more fat in our clothing and blankets than in the bacon itself, which is so thin that it is nothing but hide and hair. The men are very thin, and about worn out. Started Edwaddy and another courier for Sahuaripa and Ures to learn the true story of the various reports concerning Indian depredations in that section.

93

August 10th, 1886

Marched back to the river and camped near the old corral on the opposite side. Went down to the river to take a swim, but found the river rather swollen and dangerous in places. Distance 8 miles.

8

August 11, 1886

In camp all day, waiting for news from the south. Horn and I went out hunting, covered a good deal of ground, working hard but no luck.

While out we had a rather strange adventure, indicating undoubtedly the immediate proximity of some of the hostiles, who were probably watching our movements. We were working up a canon when suddenly a couple of bullets struck so near us that we were both covered with dirt. My mouth and face were full of it. Horn was also well covered. We dropped under cover of the nearest rocks without waiting to ask any questions. Kept under cover for some time, and finally worked back carefully under cover over the ridge. The people who fired at us must undoubtedly have been Indians on the opposite side of the canon. Distance made about 10 miles.

10

August 12th, 1886

Crossed the river and marched up Nacori Creek about 5 miles camping near our old camp.

Captain Lawton came very near dying today. We had for the morning meal a two pound can of Armour's corned beef. Lawton put the balance of the can in his saddle pocket, and just before going into camp took it out and ate some. The result was a violent attack of what seemed to be ptomaine poisoning. He became dizzy, finally unconscious, and fell from his horse. Vomiting and purging, and in a state of complete collapse.[9] We had to carry him two or three hundred feet down a steep and difficult

trail to the river, where I had a shelter built alongside the water.
By stimulating him vigorously I pulled him through the crisis,
but he was left exceedingly weak and in a bad state of collapse.
10

August 13th, 1886

Lay in camp all day, Lawton too weak to move. Indians
out today and yesterday, going over the country in all directions.
Lawton's condition changed for the better today. Aside from
weakness he is all right tonight. Weather frightfully hot, usual
rains at night. A piece of fresh meat hung up for a couple of
hours was simply filled with maggots from blow flies.

August 14th, 1886

Left camp at 6:30 A.M. and marched up the trail by our
old camp on Nacori Creek. When near our old camp we met
Benson and Long, with some mail, and instructions for Lawton,
but none for any of the rest of us. Benson had come over from
our supply camp near Oposura and made the ride in very short
time, practically alone. This was one of the many long rides he
made through the Indian country unattended. We passed
through Nacori and went into camp about 10 miles, at some
stone tanks in the rocks, where Captain Crawford and Davis[10]
had camped during the campaigns of previous years. Plenty of
wood, water and grass. Benson with us. Walsh with a grievance.
30

August 15th, 1886

Left camp at 6:00 A.M. and marched to Racaduahuachi
[Bacadéhuachi], where Benson, Chief Packer Brown, and part of
the packtrain left for Oposura to get supplies and rejoin later.
We were in town a couple of hours, and then pulled out. I was
the last officer out of town and, in fact, the last person, as Lawton had asked me to see that all the Indians were out of town
before I left. The command went on to camp about 15 miles

beyond the town, where good wood, water and grass were found. Also bought a beef and everyone had a good feed.

Shortly after leaving town I noticed that the Indians in the rear of the column were getting pretty drunk, and Horn, who was with me, went on to overtake Lawton and report the situation, as I feared from their actions that we would have trouble with them. They were very friendly with me personally, as I had hunted with them a good deal and tramped with them more or less. Soon I was surrounded with a bunch of them and asked to join in celebrating. They proposed that we should all go off and kill some Mexicans, which latter action they were very anxious to take. They wanted me to go along with them, because I could travel with them and they were all very friendly with me.

Finally, they were so threatening and drunk that I pulled out for camp to give the alarm and get assistance, as I feared they might meet and kill some Mexicans on the trail. As I was leaving I met Brown with some sober Indians and we went back together to try once more, but as the Indians were shooting at everything in sight it took some time to get them straightened out. After a while we succeeded in doing so and got them to camp. Gatewood's two Indians were exceedingly drunk and dangerous. The Indians killed one beef and one of their horses. When we got them into camp we had to tie up some of them, notably Tony, the 1st Sergeant, and a number of others. Old Jose Maria Alias and one of the Scouts had a long rough and tumble fight before we could separate them. It was a nasty time quieting this row, as the drunken men would load their arms and point them in any direction and fire, sometimes toward us and sometimes in the air. The only thing to do was wait until a man had an empty gun and then down him. The sober Indians used the butts of their guns freely. The result was a rather damaged looking lot of drunks. Fortunately no one was killed. A rather lively day. Distance marched 24 miles.

24

The Surrender

August 16th, 1886

Marched through a delightful rolling country today, with plenty of running water, grass good, and small live oak timber. In the afternoon we came up with Jim Parker's outfit who was camped here with the outfit of Nogales so-called scouts whom I mentioned early in this account,[11] a few cavalry, and quite a big outfit. Bullard, Montoya, and Dr. Bannister were in camp. Richardson was back bringing up supplies. Parker's Mexicans a worthless outfit, and of absolutely no use to anyone. Parker's camp is at a place called Weperai [Huepari], at a large old stone corral. Distance today 12 miles.

12

August 17th, 1886

My mule and horse broke out from the herd last night and it took us about an hour to find them this morning. We finally found them and started after the command, overtaking it southeast of Opoto in a hot beastly spot, almost void of water and everything else. After an hour's rest Lawton, Horn, and I went into town where we were very well received and cared for. No Indian news of definite character. Opoto is a quiet sleepy little town on the banks of a small stream.[12] Distance marched today 30 miles.

30

August 18th, 1886

We were very nicely treated while in town last night, and given a supper by one of the well-to-do men of the town. Also a breakfast this morning. Our host refused all pay. Pulled out this morning, taking a trail running a little east of north and passing through a beautiful canon full of timber. A delightful spot, with a stream of clear running water. The trail finally left th canon and ran for several miles over a rolling country, with good grass. We finally campcd on thc trail to Nacosari. Trail rough much of the way.

22

August 19th, 1886

Marched at 6:00 A.M. and made camp in a beautiful rolling country, with fine grass and good surface water. Oak trees. The camp is east of La Punca, and west of the Pinto Mountains. Many deer seen during the day. Lieutenant Spencer,[13] Corps of Engineers, came up with 5 men, having left his packs behind, animals played out. Spencer full of Indian stories. Reports seeing trails, etc.

Last night while in camp a Mexican packtrain came in from the north and reported that the Indians are near Fronteras, and that Jose Maria Alias' house was visited by some of their women during the night. They called to his wife, who understands Apache, and explained that they wanted to open up communication with him. Probably to ascertain exactly what conditions, if any, they can get from our command. They evidently expect her to communicate with him, apparently knowing we were coming north.

As soon as this news reached us yesterday, which was shortly after we got into camp, Lawton directed Gatewood to go ahead at once with his two Indians, giving him ten picked men, his two Indians, his interpreter, George Wratten, and a number of packers. Lawton's orders were for Gatewood to push rapidly into Fronteras, put his Indians on the trail to the hostile camp, and open up communication, according to orders. Gatewood packed and filled during the afternoon. He was far from well. Late in the evening Lawton came to me full of indignation because Gatewood has not yet left; he had a good mind to put him under his arrest and turn his work over to someone else. I urged him not to do this, as I believed it would only be the beginning of a long row. Finally Gatewood got off this morning, leaving after midnight. He could have gotten off yesterday evening. Lawton much annoyed and very anxious and impatient to open up communications.

We had a good swim in the pool just below camp, washed up some of our scanty clothing and dried it. Cloud burst just above camp in the mountains. Water came down the canon as a solid wall about 4 feet high, bringing with it stones, trees and everything else, After an hour or two it fell. Distance marched today 25 miles.

25

August 20th, 1886

Marched at 6:00 A.M. and went to Taracachi Ranch, 20 miles south of Fronteras. Reached camp about 11:00 A.M. and lay there all day waiting for news. Killed a couple of steers; paid $25.00 for them. Paid guide sent to us by Gatewood $6.00. Word received today that General Forsythe[14] and two troops of the 4th Cavalry is in camp 8 miles from here. Captain Wilder,[15] 4th Cavalry, is with him. Distance 15 miles.

15

August 21st, 1886

Command in camp waiting for news. Couriers coming up and down from Forsythe's camp to ours. Gatewood not heard from by us. Gave Horn $5.00 by order of Captain Lawton. Lieutenant Thomas Clay, 10th Infantry,[16] came in with the packtrain during the night. Reports that Gatewood with his two Chirachauas [sic] are not out on the trail. Clay came in from the north and passed through Fronteras or near enough to get the news.

August 22nd, 1886

Lawton, Clay, and I went up to Fronteras today, taking with us Huber and Williams. Just as we were approaching town we ran into George Ratten [Wratten], Gatewood's interpreter, and learned that Gatewood and his two Indians are in Wilder's camp and have not gone out on the trail. Lawton very angry and sent for Gatewood in post haste. I thought there was going to be a big row. On reaching Fronteras, which is a little Mexican town in Northern Sonora, we found the whole town in a turmoil of excitement. Some 60 Mexican soldiers concealed in the town. It seems that they seized the two Indian women who came in to talk with the wife of Jose Maria Alias, hoping that the hostiles would try to come in and rescue them. Wilder, as soon as he arrived and learned of the situation, insisted on their being released and sent back to their people, and attempted to send with them such general statement as would give them an idea of our policy concerning them.

Gatewood came up later on. I assumed authority to tell him that Lawton was busy and directed me to give him orders to take his Indians and immediately go out on the trail, and informed him that Lawton was extremely annoyed at his delay and the time which had been lost.[17]

Returned to camp about midnight.

40

August 23rd, 1886

We lay in camp until noon, when I went out and killed a beef, after missing a fair shot. When I returned to camp I found some Mexican soldiers camped near us. We moved up to a camp near Fronteras, and camped on a ranch 3 miles south of the town. An immense number of blow flies about camp. They simply covered our meat and filled it with eggs if it was exposed for an[y] length of time.

August 24th, 1886

The Indian Scouts under Brown went out early this morning striking to the east and south in order to cut the trail of Gatewood and his Indians and follow it up so as to be in supporting distance in case of trouble. Shortly afterwards we all left. Three of our Scouts who remained with us as guides said they did not know the country, but Lawton pushed on ahead, hoping to cut the trail of Brown and the other Indians and follow it up to where Gatewood is. We finally camped, failing to find the trail of either Gatewood or of our own Scouts under Brown. Most of the distance we came near the regular Mexican trail which runs from Fronteras to Bavispe. It was fairly good, but very little water on it.

25

August 25th, 1886

Captain Lawton, Clay, Smith, and I started ahead to attempt to cut the trail running south. The country was rapidly becoming difficult. We took with us a man who came in from Gatewood's camp yesterday. The country was very rough, and finally became so difficult that there seemed no chance of the packtrain coming further, so I was sent back to hold them, and in case no word came to go ahead and select a camp where there was grass, water and wood for their use. Lawton, Smith and a few men, some ten in all, kept on. Took one back with me.

After waiting a time we camped at a point about 8 miles from our camp of yesterday. We had hardly gotten the packs off when a courier came in from Lawton with orders to march on to the Indian trail tonight, so we packed up and marched back to a point about 2 miles from our camp of yesterday, from which point we could strike the trail of our Scouts and follow it in the morning. The reason we did do this when we started out this morning was simply because we did not know that the Scouts, being on foot, would take such country that we could follow them with the packs. Hence we started out through what seemed to be the most passable country with the result that we were soon tied up. It seems that about half an hour after leaving Lawton he struck the Indian trail and wanted us to follow it with as little delay as practicable, in order that his whole command might be concentrated. That is to say, the whole outfit join Brown and the Scouts, who are on ahead with Gatewood and his Indians.

16

Chasing Geronimo

August 26th, 1886

Last night after getting into camp and fixing up everything for an early move, we built a good sized camp fire made some tea and had a good supper, as we all felt sure there was a hard day's work ahead, and that something was going to happen. When we woke up this morning we found the B Troop's horses missing. The herd had become frightened during the night and had scattered badly. Walsh was so broken up that he sat down and cried like a baby. At 9:00 A.M., by hard work and much riding, we had all the horses together and were about to start when Billy Long came in with a note from Lawton saying he wanted six mules, lightly loaded with rations and some tobacco started at once and rushed through, and that he trusted me to do it. The man stated that Lieutenant Smith had started with him and was back a little in the hills, and would soon be in. That his animal was tired and was coming slowly. We sent a man out, who fired some shots and finally got a reply from Smith.

The mules were loaded and Smith and I, with two packers, and an Indian, started. We had an exceedingly hard time, the trail was rough, sodden, and the ground was soft in places. When we struck the Indian trail it was exceedingly rough and the heavy rain made the going very difficult and at places washed out badly so that it was hard to follow. We pushed on as fast as we could and kept it up until after midnight. The last hour or two we made a little headway. We were up in the mountains, with high cliffs and sharp fall offs. No stars or moon. We tried for an hour or so to follow the trail by lighting matches, everything else was to [too] wet to burn.

Finally we had to go into camp, as the rain began to fall in torrents. Tied up our animals to the loads. Put riggings, aparejos, together and got in under them, each of us climbing in under three riggings put in line. A nasty mess. Some of the mules had sore backs, and everything was soaked with sweat. We finally decided it was better to lie out in the rain. Nothing to eat but a few crackers. Packers and mules very tired.

Chapter 6: *The Problems of Negotiation and Surrender*

"I feel sure from the fact that [the Indians] will march to the United States that they are earnest in their desire to come in. I am pretty tired and feel the strain of responsibility weighing on me. . . . I feel strongly my situation and how much depends on . . . the action of General Miles and his approval or disapproval of my action."

"I cannot get Miles to come out and the Indians are uneasy about it."

Lawton to Mame, August 27, September 2, 1886

August 27th, 1886

Pulled out at daybreak and moved forward as rapidly as possible. Reached the river shortly after light, and found the outfit camped on the San Bernardino. Expect the Indians in for a talk. If we had had two hours more of daylight we could have reached camp. Had some trouble in crossing the stream, as it was very high and swift, and exceedingly difficult to cross. Found our outfit hard up for rations, they had eaten very little, but had eaten a mule which was killed last night by one of the scouts. This is the first mule meat they have eaten on the trip.

Some of Geronimo's Indians were in camp yesterday and a few of them were down at the river near where we crossed this morning at daybreak, but were afraid to try it. They came again later, and we managed to get some rations across to them. Sent an Indian back for my belt which I left just across the river near our last night's camp. He was rather afraid to go back near the hostiles. Paid him $4.00 for making the trip. At noon we moved up the creek two miles toward San Bernardino and camped directly across the stream from the hostile camp.

In the afternoon Geronimo, Natchez, and most of the outfit came over. Natchez is the hereditary chief and real leader.[1] Geronimo is the man who always appears. Had a long talk, during which all arrangements for surrendering to us and going with us to Skeleton Canon[2] were gone over and agreed to. I wrote some letters and got them off by Edwaddy and Wilson, who were sent north with information of the surrender. Wilson went by way of Richardson's camp (4th Cavalry) at Fronteras, and Edwaddy direct.

Indians anxious to go in with us to surrender. Geronimo stated: "We have not slept for six months and are worn out" and stated that he and his party were tired out and anxious to join their relatives in Florida. All they seemed to dread especially was falling into the hands of the civil authorities in Arizona. They were anxious to have us move up with them. Geronimo stayed in camp until we had our dinner in which he joined us, eating heartily of everything. The Indians are literally worn out with anxiety and hard travelling. They have been constantly on the watch, frequently attacked, and have again and again had close calls. Natchez looks thin, and has not entirely recovered from a wound received several weeks ago in a fight with some American ranchers down near Cumpas. A heavy rain during the afternoon.

There were no definite terms offered the Indians at this time. They were told that General Miles sent word that he would use every possible effort to send them promptly out of Arizona and to save their lives.

10

August 28th, 1886
Moved this morning very early, all feeling cheerful as we

realized that one of the longest, if not the longest, march after hostiles in the history of our army, was at an end, or nearly so. Early in the afternoon some of the hostile Indians reported that they had seen from their camp a number of Mexican soldiers crossing the mountains several miles below us. We could also plainly make them out, coming over in a long line, dressed in white, seemed to be all infantry. A tremendous amount of excitement in the hostile camp and some in ours, as the packers piled the packs into breastworks and the scouts began to throw up small stone breastworks about us. Everyone was on the move getting ready for whatever might turn up, on the whole rather hoping that there would be a fight and thereby have a chance to even up with the Mexicans for poor Crawford's death. Lawton sent out word to Smith and myself to go down and meet the Mexicans as quickly as possible. I happened to be the nearest ready and started off at once on a mule; Smith and Horn followed immediately afterwards.

We met them coming in a single file through a dense canebrake. Had a long talk with them and told them if they came on there would be a fight, that both the hostile Indians and ourselves were united and in a position to attack them as they came out of the canebrake. In the meantime Smith had started back to bring Lawton down. I had on nothing but a pair of canton flannel drawers, an old blue blouse, a pair of mocassins and a hat without any crown, and I do not blame the Mexican commander for not believing I was an officer. However, he evidently did not want a fight and finally they all halted, but in a very ugly mood. Horn and I kept them busy talking until finally Lawton came; then the interview assumed a more formal aspect.

The Mexicans were told that the Indians had surrendered to us, and that we would not permit them to be interfered with, and that any attempt to interfere with them or arrest them meant a fight with us. There were 180 Mexicans, all armed with Remingtons, led by the Prefect of Arispe, the same gentleman Lawton and I met at Fronteras a few days ago. The Mexicans wanted the Indians themselves, wanted to take them for alleged crimes in Sonora, which I have no doubt they committed. As soon as Lawton had laid down the proposition to the Mexicans and it was evident that they were not going to molest any of us or fight, either, Lawton sent me up to the hostile camp with a message to the effect that he would protect them at all hazards.

Geronimo and Natchez in the meantime had sent word over to our camp that they were all ready for a fight and would attack the Mexicans in the rear as soon as the fight opened up. I have no doubt we could have cleaned up the whole bunch without heavy loss. As soon as I had reached our camp I found that the Indian camp had moved out, and with Gatewood and Walsh were moving northward towards the United States. I followed as fast as possible. While following them up, one or two of the hostiles jumped up from behind a boulder along the trail, where they had evidently been lying as a rear guard. They joined me and trotted on. They were so well covered up that I did not see them until well on them. They could easily have shot me. This move was in response to an order of Lawton's given as he started to come down to talk with the Mexicans. His idea was to get the hostiles out of the way.

After several hours of hard riding I overtook the Indians in camp and gave them the message and assurances from Lawton. After explaining the situation to them fully I rode back and met Lawton and the outfit and told him that the Indians were much excited and had asked that no Mexicans be allowed to come on with him, that they should be sent back and not allowed to come into camp. Lawton compromised by keeping them in the rear of his party. We went into camp a short distance from the Indian camp.

After a little, Geronimo and some of his Indians came down to visit our camp. The Mexicans were standing with Lawton, myself, Clay and other of our officers. They rather lost their nerve as Geronimo and Natchez approached and one or two of them pulled their revolvers around. In an instant the Indians had them covered with their rifles, and Lawton, Clay and myself jumped between the two parties, fearing the Mexicans would be killed in our camp. We had no fear for the Indians. It was the Prefect of Arispe who commenced fidgeting with his gun, and upset the nerves of his fellow officers. After this incident the Mexican officers left for their own camp, quite satisfied with their experience. Gatewood and George Ratten [Wratten] stayed in the Indian camp to re-assure them. The camp was adjoining ours.

24

August 29th, 1886

Captain Lawton, Clay and I moved out on the trail of the hostile Indians, who had broken camp early, and followed to their camp, leaving Smith in command of the main column. We had with us our orderlies only. The Indians received us as pleasantly as could be expected; we waited for an hour or two for the arrival of the main command, then sent George Williams, my orderly, after the packtrain and Smith, which had apparently lost the trail, having followed up the San Bernardino Creek instead of swinging off and taking our line of march.

After an hour or two more Captain Lawton started out to search for the command. Neither returned, and Gatewood, Clay, and I, with Captain Lawton's orderly, Huber, remained in camp all night. We were very decently treated and given the best they had. George Ratten had gone with Lawton or just before him to look for the packtrain, none of them returned that night. Toward night we moved camp, marched about 8 miles, the Indians selecting a very defensible position for their camp and scattering over a large area. No shelters put up. Slept in the wet grass.

20

August 30th, 1886

At daybreak we moved and marched 8 miles to the Alias Creek and camped on good water. It has been rather a novel experience, this travelling with the hostiles. They were all fully armed and could have seized us at any time as hostages. Natchez came to me last night and said to me, "You are in our camp, but our camp is your camp, and you can be here just as at home."

We lay in camp on Alias Creek all day. Toward 10:00 A.M. I pulled out and struck across country to the old pack trail of Maus, and found all our outfit camped 5 miles south of Bernardine Ranch. Captain Lawton had just gone into the ranch to send a heliographic[3] message. Smith was in command of the camp. The outfit moved out very shortly after my arrival. Left word for Lawton where to join and marched to the hostile camp. Camped about ¼ mile from them on good grass. Courier came in today bringing some mail.

30

August 31st, 1886

Command left camp this morning at 7:00 A.M. with the hostiles, who are marching directly ahead of the main command. Lieut. Richards[4] overtook us about 3 miles from camp and brought word from Lawton, who is still at San Bernardino. Camped in Guadalupe canon.[5] Found very little water, just enough to make coffee. The Indians had misunderstood the remarks of Lt. Smith which they overheard in a conversation in which he had apparently spoken of the possibility of surrounding them in case they tried to break loose. The Indians were a good deal excited as they approached the frontier, and whatever they heard excited them very much more. Smith ranked Gatewood one file,[6] and rather sharp friction developed between them this morning. The Indians knew Gatewood and did not know Smith. As a result I sent my orderly for Lawton with word that the situation was bad and to get into camp as soon as he could. Lawton came in, having used up his horse in making the trip. He was much excited and annoyed as he feared the Indians had left us. As a matter of fact, the Indians had moved out some distance. Lawton and I, with some of our orderlies, followed them and went into their camp which we reached about 8:00 P.M. We reassured them, and told them everything was all right. Lawton had a long talk with them. Had our supper with the Indians. The Indians were greatly excited today, and it would have taken very little to have sent them out as wild as ever.[7]

15

September 1st, 1886

We moved out of camp this morning and went about 2 miles up the canon to an old ranch near some big cottonwood trees where there is good water and grass. The hostiles camped near us. In the afternoon Richards came into camp, also Parker, Bannister, and Bullard. Everyone delighted at the prospect of the campaign soon being closed.

3

September 2nd, 1886

Lay in camp until this afternoon and then pulled out for a ranch about 12 miles distant in Skeleton Canon. Reached camp about dark. Hostiles in camp, about 1½ miles from us. Captain Foote[8] and Dr. Anderson came into camp from their command somewhere near us.

12

September 3rd, 1886

A perfect epidemic of couriers. No news. Everybody trying to do something and doing nothing. General Miles and staff came into camp at 3:00 P.M. Geronimo came down and had a long talk with him, also some of his Indians. Natchez did not come down; he was out looking for his brother, who is not with the band, but believed to be in this section somewhere. Lt. Wilder and Lt. Amcs[9] came in with General Miles, also Dapray. A long talk this afternoon between the Indians and General Miles.

September 4th, 1886

In camp all day. Much talking going on. Natchez came down, and all is well. Jose Maria Alias acting rather ugly and causing some trouble. Surrender to be arranged today. No meat in camp; went out after some beef with Natchez. Killed a couple of fine steers. Made a very curious shot. Natchez had gotten around behind some cattle and was driving them towards me. I fired at a fine steer, shot him through the neck, killing him; the bullet went on (the old 500 grain 45 caliber) passed through the brain of a steer just on the other side, killing it. This steer jumped straight into the air, and falling on a yearling cow broke her back. Natchez very much amused; he knew at once what had happened. As the herd moved off I saw instead of one three beef. We killed the calf to put it out of its suffering. As a result, we had plenty of beef in camp that night.

September 5th, 1886

General Miles left camp this morning with Natchez and Geronimo, an Indian named Perico, two other men, and also a squaw. They are going to push on, driving hard, and hope to reach Fort Bowie. Clay also went along, riding the mule. About 75 miles to make. Our command moved along leisurely, starting out at 3:00 P.M. and marched across to the foothills of the Chirachua Mountains, where we found a camp on good water. Everything peaceful today. Indians travelling along quietly near our command. The Scouts and hostiles march as two distinct bodies.

15

September 6th, 1886

Marched to Cave Creek and had dinner. Pulled out again at 3:00 P.M. and marched to Gilaville, and went into camp. Had a lovely camp.

15

September 7th, 1886

Marched from camp to a ranch 14 miles distant, and

camped on good water for a few hours. Water in tanks. Heavy showers. Indians going along all right. Marched on again and camped for the night near Bowie.

Yesterday, while on the march, a young Indian girl gave birth to a child. The command halted perhaps an hour for this purpose and then took up the march, the girl carrying her young baby. She looked pretty pale, but otherwise seemed to pay little attention to the incident.

19

September 8th, 1886

Last night three bucks, one of them a brother of Natchez, a fairly well grown boy, and three women, left camp. Their departure took place toward morning, and was undoubtedly due to the foolish conduct of Lieutenant Ames. Captain Lawton had given orders that no one was to come to our camp before daybreak, knowing that the Indians were excited and alarmed and feared that some of them, especially those charged with crimes in Arizona, would fear that someone was coming out to arrest them and light out. Ames started out from Bowie long before light and rode into our camp on a big white horse at a run. Nothing more idiotic could be imagined. I have always believed he was nervous and anxious to get in among white troops. It had been raining during the night and was still very dark when he came in. The Indians scattered, and when we got them together again we found the above mentioned Indians missing.

We arrived at Fort Bowie, rapidly arranged for the transportation of the troops to Bowie station, secured such stores as were necessary for the journey, gave the Indians an opportunity to get such clothing as they wanted; I got hold of some of my clothing which had been sent to Bowie, including my trunk, but had no time to change. Some photographs were made in Bowie of the Indians, some of which I have ordered.

About 11:00 A.M. we were ready to move. The Indians were put in escort wagons, escorted by cavalry, and were transferred at a rapid pace to the station, where a train had been waiting since early morning. Reached the station at 1:30 and immediately pulled out. General Miles and staff accompanied us. On the way down, [William A.] Thompson, Acting Assistant Adjutant General, said to me, patting his pocket and acting under the confidence bred by several drinks and old friendship: "I have got something here which would stop this movement, but I am not going to let the old man see it until you are gone, then I will repeat it to him."[10] He had orders from Washington not to permit the Indians to leave Arizona, but I knew that if he acted on this no end of confusion would result. All of us went down to Bowie station on horseback. Some local photographer took a snap of us. I was mounted on a grey horse at the end of the line. Ordered some of the photographs as souvenirs. The Indians were promptly put on the train and the train left for San Antonio, Texas, General Miles and staff travelling with us as far as the New Mexican border.

Epilogue

We terminated the campaign and General Miles seems inclined to do all he can for those of us who did hard work. . . .

Wood to Jake, September 16, 1886

The work of the expedition ended when the Indians arrived at Fort Bowie; but the successful capture of Geronimo's band created the new problem of disposition of the Apaches. During July and August, Miles transferred most of the Chiricahuas to Fort Marion, Florida, and he wanted to send Geronimo's band to join them. Miles planned to make the transfer of Geronimo and his band a part of his surrender terms. But when he made his views known to Washington, complications arose. The Indians, he was told, were to be treated not as belligerents but as outlaws. They were to be given no terms, and because President Grover Cleveland had not made up his mind about the disposition of the hostiles, they were to be held at Fort Bowie.[1]

The news that Geronimo had surrendered to the expedition on August 27 placed Miles in a serious quandary: Geronimo had been told that he would receive safe conduct out of Arizona, and now that the band had agreed to negotiate, Miles had no terms to offer him. Lawton had assured the Indian chief on the 27th that Miles would meet with him. But with no terms except unconditional surrender, Miles began to vacillate, at one time leaving Lawton with the impression that he would meet with Geronimo and at another instructing his commander to treat the

Indians as hostages. Wood's Journal does not indicate the tension which permeated the expedition during the journey northward from August 28 to September 2. Lawton had by no means captured the Indians. They were still armed, they marched northward in a line independent of the expedition, and they made their own camp at night—all of which made it possible for them to vanish at any time they chose. The absence of Miles made the Indians extremely restless as the expedition neared the Mexican-Arizona border. Lawton was beside himself: "I cannot get Miles to come out and see them and they are very uneasy about it," he complained to his wife. "What will occur no one can tell."[2]

Finally, just as the expedition crossed over the border, Miles decided to ignore Washington's directive and to negotiate with Geronimo. As this was a direct violation of orders he had received earlier, Miles needed to act quickly to present the government with a *fait accompli*. The Indians were rushed to Fort Bowie, arriving there on September 8. They were "put in escort wagons . . . and were transferred at a rapid pace to the station, where a train had been waiting since early morning."[3] Wood records in his journal that on the way to the station, Miles' assistant adjutant general showed him a telegram from Washington ordering Miles to hold the Indians at Fort Bowie. He was withholding it from "the old man," he said, until the Indians were safely on their way to Florida.

Such a story makes for good melodrama, but Miles knew very well that he was violating orders when he first began negotiating with Geronimo. He had been told many times not only to offer the Indians no terms, but also to incarcerate them until they were tried for their crimes. On September 7, Sheridan telegraphed Miles specifically instructing him to hold the Indians at Fort Bowie, and again on September 8, Adjutant General Hugh A. Drum issued the same instructions, quoting Cleveland as stating that "Geronimo and the rest of the hostiles should be immediately sent to the nearest fort or prison where they can be securely confined."[4]

It was probably Drum's telegram that Wood saw. But even if Miles had received the telegram, his decision would not have changed. He understood Washington's views on the disposition of the Indians, but he had already decided to put them on a train for Florida. Then he would inform the government they were on their way.

At first Miles attempted to defend his violation of orders by claiming that he had received a telegram on September 4 from the Acting Secretary of War in Washington instructing him to send Geronimo to Fort Marion.[5] But Drum could find no record of such a telegram on September 4 "or any other date." "No such order," he stated flatly, "has been given."[6] Having failed to "manufacture" an order, Miles sought refuge in an interpretation of the orders given him. The basis for Geronimo's transfer, he then argued, was the President's order to send the Indians to the nearest fort where they could be "securely confined." Miles contended that he did not have the troops to "securely confine" them in Arizona; had he not acted when he did, they would have escaped. To turn them over to the local civilian authorities, he claimed with some justification, would have been a "mockery of justice." "In order to carry out the orders of the President, it was an imperative necessity to remove the entire tribe to a place of safety."[7] Ostensibly, the nearest place of safety was Fort Marion, Florida.

Mainly because the government's demands were so unrealistic, Miles's coup was successful. Few officers would have been willing to chance Miles's not uncharacteristic insubordination (although the more militarily correct Crook came very near it before he asked to be relieved);[8] yet many department commanders found policy made in Washington not only unsuited to local conditions but virtually impossible to implement. At times, as with the case of Crook, policy made by local commanders was found unacceptable in Washington, even when it had been generally successful. The powers in government, from the commanding general to the President, seemed to have little comprehension of the difficulties of Indian warfare in the Southwest. Sheridan, who should have known better, found it difficult to understand why Crook could not cover his entire territory with forty-six companies of infantry and forty of cavalry.[9] He never really understood why Miles found it so difficult to round up a small band of Indians and to lock them up in Fort Bowie or some other place until the government decided on their disposition. Miles' explanation that Geronimo if not given safe conduct out of Arizona, preferred to die in the Sierra Madre Mountains rather than at the hands of the United States government seemed to have little effect. Miles' decision to transport the Indians to Florida, though undoubtedly insubordinate, was probably a correct one under the conditions prevailing there at the time. It probably saved the government much trouble later on.

The government made one last futile effort to control the disposition of the Apaches by stopping the train in San Antonio in order, as one writer noted, to clear "the fog which appeared to lie over the final act of surrender."[10] Cleveland directed the department commander at San Antonio to confer with Geronimo to find out exactly what was promised him in Skeleton Canyon. Geronimo confirmed that Miles had indeed promised that the Indians would join their families. The train continued to Florida.[11]

Much praise was heaped upon those responsible for the surrender of Geronimo and his exile to Florida. Miles included Wood in the territory's celebration in their honor during the next several weeks. In their official reports both Lawton and Miles were generous in their praise of Wood. Lawton was particularly effusive. Wood, he reported, was the only officer with him throughout the entire campaign:

> His courage, energy, and loyal support during the whole time; his encouraging example to the command, when work was hardest and prospects darkest; his thorough confidence and belief in the final success of the expedi-

tion, his untiring efforts to make it so, has placed me
under obligation so great that I cannot express them.[12]

He cited Wood's work not only as a medical officer of the command, but also his services as combatant line officer, since in the
midst of the campaign Wood had voluntarily assumed command
of the Infantry company.

In 1898, of all the officers who had served in the long campaign
against the Apaches, Wood was singled out to receive the Medal
of Honor. The citation read:

> Throughout the campaign against the hostile Apaches
> in the summer of 1886, this officer, serving as Medical
> Officer with Captain Lawton's expedition, rendered spe-
> cifically courageous and able services involving extreme
> peril and display of most conspicuous gallantry under
> conditions of great danger, hardships and privations. He
> volunteered to carry dispatches through a region infested
> with hostile Indians, making a journey of seventy miles
> in one night and then marched thirty miles on foot the
> next day. For several weeks, while in close pursuit of
> Geronimo's band and constantly expecting an encounter,
> Assistant Surgeon Wood exercised the command of a
> detachment of Infantry to which he requested assign-
> ment and that was without an officer.[13]

The award was a bitter pill for the other officers who had
campaigned for years against the Apaches. It was bad enough
for Crook and his men to find, after long years of fighting and
working to pacify the Apaches, that Miles and his men received
the glory and subsequent benefits for ending the Apache threat.[14]
The lone Crook man involved in the final surrender of Geronimo
was Charles Gatewood. The sickly lieutenant, who suffered
mightily in the final days of the campaign and who had played
a large role in Geronimo's surrender, received little or no benefits for his work. While Miles, Lawton, and Wood realized one

advancement after another, Gatewood sank into obscurity. He served as Miles' aide for four years and was then ordered out on another Indian campaign in 1890. Injured in a post explosion he retired as a first lieutenant. He died in 1896.[15]

Then in 1898, when there were so many line officers who might have been rewarded, the government chose to award a Medal of Honor to a doctor in the Medical Corps, an award many thought should have gone to Gatewood. Wood's citation became, as one campaign officer wrote with considerable sarcasm and understatement, "the subject of considerable discussion."[16] The opposition it aroused followed Wood throughout his military career.

Whether Wood should have been singled out over a Gatewood, a Lawton, or a Crawford for such an honor is debatable. What cannot be contested was Wood's courage, energy, and endurance during the campaign. There seems to be no reason to doubt Lawton's sincerity when he praised Wood's essential contribution to the expedition. In any case, it was a splendid way to begin a career; it portended more honors in the future.

Notes

INTRODUCTION

[1] Robert M. Utley. *Frontiersmen in Blue, 1848-1865.* (New York, 1967). Chapter 3.

[2] Russell F. Weigley. *History of the United States Army.* (New York, 1967). 267 and Appendix.

[3] Quoted in Oliver Spaulding, *The United States Army in War and Peace.* (New York, 1937). 362.

[4] John G. Bourke. *On The Border With Crook.* (New York, 1891). 329.

[5] Martin F. Schmitt, ed., *General Crook, His Autobiography.* (Norman, Oklahoma, 1960). 244-250. Captain Emmet Crawford and Lt. Charles Gatewood were attached to the Indians as military agents. See Britton Davis, *The Truth About Geronimo.* (New Haven, 1929), Chapter 9 for a description of the military administration of the Apaches at the San Carlos Reservation.

[6] Schmitt, *General Crook,* 263-264; Davis, *Geronimo,* 221-222.

[7] Schmitt, *General Crook,* 251-266.

[8] Edward Ransom, "Nelson A. Miles as Commanding General, 1895-1903," *Military Affairs,* XXIX (Winter, 1965-66), 180.

[9] Virginia W. Johnson, *The Unregimented General: A Biography of Nelson A. Miles* (Boston, 1962), 229; Nelson A. Miles, *Serving the Republic.* (New York, 1911), 221.

[10] Johnson, *Unregimented General,* 236.

[11] Report of Secretary of War, *Annual Report* (1886), 72.

[12] R. R. Drum to Miles, April 3, 1886. Senate Document No. 117. 49th Congress, 2nd Session, "The Surrender of Geronimo," 1886-1887.

[13] Fairfax Downey, *Indian-Fighting Army.* (New York, 1941), 279.

[14] Miles to Sheridan, July 7, 1886. National Archives, Adjutant General's Office, Record Group 94, File 1550.

[15] Diary entry October 31, 1885. Leonard Wood Papers. Library of Congress.

[16] Diary, March 26, June 2, 1886.

[17] The officer was Robert Lee Bullard. See footnote 8, Chapter 5, for a

more detailed discussion. See also Hermann Hagedorn's interviews with Thomas Clay (1929) and R. A. Brown (1929). Hagedorn Papers. Library of Congress.

[18] Lawton Papers. Library of Congress.

[19] Wood to Jake, July 6, 1885. Wood Papers. Library of Congress. For Wood's desire to become a regular officer, see James Parker, *The Old Army*. (New York, 1929), 168.

[20] Wood to Jake, July 26, 1885. Wood Papers.

[21] See *Diary* entry May 4, 1886. Later, Wood wrote his brother, (as the Mexican campaign proved, with not much exaggeration): "I am in first rate health and can run with the Indian Scouts all day and be fresh as ever the next morning." Wood to Jake, June 1, 1886. Wood Papers.

[22] Colonel William Royall to Lawton, Senate Document No. 117, "Surrender of Geronimo," 45.

[23] Lawton to Mame, July 14, 1886. Lawton Papers, Library of Congress.

[24] *Ibid.*, July 22, 1886.

[25] *Ibid.*, July 17, 1886.

[26] The main source for this is James Parker, who reported that when Lawton was told of Gatewood's mission he replied: "I get my orders from President Cleveland. I am ordered to hunt Geronimo down and kill him. I cannot treat with him." Quoted in Davis, *Geronimo*, 229.

This story does not completely accord with Wood's Diary nor Lawton's letters to his wife. On August 22, 1886, he wrote his wife: "I will do all I can for Gatewood by making it hot for Geronimo." Possibly Parker's story does represent Lawton's first reaction. He may have been "letting off steam," as one writer has suggested. Hermann Hagedorn, *Leonard Wood, A Biography*, I. (New York, 1931), 85.

[27] Lawton to Mame, August 27, 1886. Lawton Papers.

[28] *Ibid.*

[29] Hagedorn, *Wood*, I, 101.

[30] George Crook, "The Apache Problem," *Journal of the Military Service Institution of the United States*, VII. (October, 1886).

[31] John G. Bourke, *On the Border With Crook*. (New York, 1891).

[32] Nelson A. Miles, *Personal Recollections and Observations of General A. Miles*. (Chicago, 1896); *Serving With the Republic: Memoirs of the Civil and Military Life of Nelson A. Miles*. (New York, 1911).

[33] James Parker, *The Old Army Memories*. (Philadelphia, 1929).

[34] Britton Davis, *Geronimo*. (New York, 1929).

[35] Robert Utley, "Foreword" in Davis, *Geronimo*. (New Haven, 1963), xviii.

[36] *Ibid.*, xix.

Notes

CHAPTER 1

[1] Davis and Crawford were two of Crook's most trusted officers. Crawford was killed while leading a contingent of Apache scouts deep into Mexico on the trail of a large group of Chiricahua Apaches. His expedition was intercepted by a force of Mexican militia who mistook the scouts for hostiles and began firing on them. Interpreters succeeded in bringing about a halt to the firing and Crawford climbed on a high rock in full view of the Mexicans to show that he was an American officer. According to Lt. Marion Maus, Crawford's aide, a Mexican standing approximately thirty yards from Crawford deliberately raised his rifle and shot the commander in the head.

Crawford's death was a severe blow to Crook and his policy. Although Maus arranged a conference between the Apache chiefs and General Crook, where the Indians agreed to surrender, Geronimo and a band of forty escaped. The combination of Crawford's death and Crook's failure to bring in all the Apaches caused serious concern in the War Department about the efficacy of Crook's policy.

Wood's estimate that Crook was "discouraged" appears generally correct; however, Crook was not, as Wood implies, convinced his policy was a failure. Sheridan was concerned because Crook was too "wedded to the policy of operating exclusively with Indian scouts." Sheridan had concluded that not only were the scouts reluctant to fight their brothers, but they were probably untrustworthy. The commanding general had already decided to reassign him when Crook, "to relieve embarrassment," asked to be relieved.

For a detailed report on Crawford's death see National Archives, The Adjutant General's Office, Record Group 94, File 1098, and Report of the Secretary of War, *Annual Report*, 1886, "Report of the Lieutenant-General of the Army." For a defense of Crook's policy see Martin Schmitt, ed., *General George Crook, His Autobiography* (Norman, Okla., 1960); Britton Davis, *The Truth About Geronimo* (New Haven, 1963), John Bourke, *On the Border With Crook* (New York, 1891).

The Mexicans presented an altogether different story about Crawford's death. They claimed Crawford's scouts attacked them first. See the correspondence between the American State Department and the Mexican government in House Executive Documents, "Foreign Relations with Mexico, 1886-1887," Vol. VII, 49th Cong., 2nd Sess., 570-691.

[2] William Shafter entered the Army in 1861 as a first lieutenant in the 7th Michigan Infantry. He was granted the Medal of Honor for gallantry at the Battle of Fair Oaks and later rose to colonel in command of the 17th United States Negro Infantry. After the Civil War he was appointed lieutenant colonel and later colonel in the Regular Army. He became brigadier

Chasing Geronimo

general in 1897 and less than one year later was selected as commander of
the Fifth Army Corps at Tampa, Florida. He led this contingent in the invasion of Cuba in June, 1898. He retired from active service in 190L Dumas Malone, *Dictionary of American Biography*, XVII, (New York, 1932),
15-16. For a cogent evaluation of Shafter, why he was selected in 1898,
and his command abilities see Margaret Leech, *In the Days of McKinley*
(New York, 1959), 202-204.

[3] Fort Bowie was at the north end of the Chiricahua Mountains, near
Apache Pass, fifteen miles southeast of Bowie Station on the Southern
Pacific Railroad. Bowie was traditionally an area of Apache depredations.
It had been Cochise's favorite stronghold. Miles claimed that when he
arrived at Fort Bowie in April, 1886, "the citizens and settlers located in
that district were the most terror-stricken people" he had ever seen. Ter-
rorized by the Apaches, they had abandoned all mines and settlements.
Nelson A. Miles, *Personal Recollections* (Chicago, 1896), 477; Schmitt,
Crook, 164: Will C. Barnes, *Arizona Place Names* (Tucson, 1935), 59.

[4] Daly was a well-known packer in the Southwest who had served with the
ill-fated Crawford expedition. He later wrote a highly inaccurate article on
his experiences with the Army. H. W. Daly, "Geronimo Campaign," *Arizona Historical Review*, III, (1930-31), 26-44.

[5] This is an understatement. Crook, with his forceful, engaging personality,
generated loyalty in about the same proportion as Miles created enemies.
When the Lawton expedition seemed bogged down deep in Mexico, Crook
was reported as saying that Miles had made a "dead failure of this [expedi-
tion] as he has every other campaign." Quoted in Johnson, *Unregimented
General*, 240.

[6] The post was Fort Huachuca. It was established in 1877 at the northern
end of the Huachuca Mountains, twelve miles from the Mexican border, as
a part of a system of posts designed to guard the border and settlers from
the Apaches. Miles moved his headquarters from Fort Bowie to Huachuca
when he arrived in 1886. It then became a center of activity but rapidly declined after the capture of Geronimo. Barnes, *Arizona Place Names*, 214;
Schmitt, *Crook*, 245; Federal Writers Project, *Arizona: A State Guide* (New
York, 1940), 300.

[7] Wood assiduously indentified the ranches they encountered in this
sparsely settled area because they were landmarks. Most of them are un-
identifiable today. But to call them ranches stretches the usual meaning of
the term. They were often nothing more than crude adobe huts occupied by
prospectors or suppliers of relay animals for stage routes. One traveller described them as "wretched forbidding-looking places . . ." with "never a
tree or a bush to give shade, nor a sign of comfort of home." Martha Summerhayes, *Vanished Arizona* (Chicago, 1939), 63.

Notes

Still these "ranches" did provide the only haven, however unsatisfactory, from the dust and burning heat. Water, always precious, was usually available, and some ranches even had a bar. Army contingents on campaigns often camped near these ranches.

The Tevis Ranch was owned by James H. Tevis, who fought with the Texans in their invasion of New Mexico during the Civil War. His memoirs were published under the title *Arizona in the '50s* (Albuquerque: New Mexico University Press, 1954).

[8] As a kind of scientific investigation to determine a white man's physical endurance in Indian country, Wood meticulously recorded the number of miles he marched daily. Specifically, Miles asked Wood to determine if the best soldiers "could not equal in activity and endurance the Apache warriors." Nelson Miles, *Serving the Republic* (New York, 1911), 224. "I would like to have you accompany Captain Lawton's command," Miles told Wood, "and as you are probably in as good condition as anyone to endure what they endure, you can make a careful study of the Indians . . . and discover wherein lies the superiority, if it does exist. . . ." Miles, *Personal Recollections*, 224.

[9] Elgin Station was a small town on a tributary of the Santa Cruz River, serving the Southern Pacific branch line from Calabasas to Benson.

[10] In addition to his duties as assistant post surgeon, Wood, like other frontier Army doctors, was expected to serve the civilian settlers and ranchers.

[11] Crittenden was located six miles north of Nogales on the Nogales to Benson branch of the Southern Pacific Railroad.

[12] Nogales was a frontier customs town on the Sonora Railroad. The name is derived from the Spanish term "nogal," meaning walnut. The first settlers claimed the Santa Cruz River was lined with walnut trees. Although originally called the Line City and then Isaactown (after a manager of a cattle company there), it was renamed Nogales in 1882. Barnes, *Arizona Place Names*, 221-223; H. H. Bancroft, *History of Arizona and New Mexico* (San Francisco, 1889), 301; Phyllis Balestrero, "Nogales," *Arizona Highways*, XXXIV (September, 1958), 8-15.

[13] T. C. Lebo was a respected veteran of several Apache campaigns. In 1886 he was commanding the all-black 10th Cavalry (the same regiment John Pershing later commanded, from which he gained the name "Black Jack"). In the first encounter with Geronimo's band after its escape in 1886, Lebo caught a small group of the hostiles in the Pinto Mountains of Sonora on May 5. One soldier was killed and another, Corporal Scott, was injured. Lebo claimed he killed eight Apaches, though they were never found and Britton Davis denied it. Davis, *Geronimo*, 219; Dan Thrapp, *The Conquest of Apachería* (Norman, Okla., 1967), 351. The most recent work on the

10th Cavalry is William Leckie, *The Buffalo Soldiers.* (Norman, Okla., 1967.)

[14] Clarke was the son of a professor at Baltimore City College. He graduated from West Point in 1884, and served primarily in the Southwest. He died prematurely in 1891. In the Lebo battle, Clarke distinguished himself by saving Corporal Scott after the latter had been wounded. Miles singled him out for bravery in a general order. Headquarters, Department of Arizona, *General Orders,* no. 12, October 7, 1886. (Copy in Wood Papers). Young Frederic Remington, who had just arrived in the Department of Arizona, interviewed Scott who told him that " 'D' at 'ar Lt. Clarke is a—fightin' man, you'd better believe". Harold McCracken, ed., *Frederic Remington's Own West* (New York, 1961), 23.

[15] Lawton constantly complained to Miles that Benson, though he meant well, was too young and immature to command. Lawton to Miles, May 12, 14, 21, 1886. Lawton Papers, Library of Congress.

[16] Hardtack and bacon or salt pork were the standard campaign ration. Pork was usually carried in a mess kit ("meat can"). As Wood often complains, intense heat almost always melted the fat portion of the pork. Improvements in rations in the 1880s added canned beans and tomatoes. Canned beef—which after the Spanish-American War Miles called "embalmed beef"—was introduced in the mid-1880's but nearly everyone complained of its sickening appearance. Later in the campaign Lawton ate some of this beef several hours after opening the can and almost died from poison. See journal entry for August 12. For an excellent description of Army food ration after the Civil War, see Don Rickey, Jr., *Forty Miles a Day on Beans and Hay* (Norman, Okla., 1963), 249.

[17] Ordinarily, shooting of game on a campaign was strictly forbidden. But this was an unorthodox expedition, and hunting to supplement the diet became essential. Ibid, 253.

[18] Approximately thirty-five miles due south of the border town of Nogales.

[19] On a railroad that ran from Nogales southward through the Sonora Province and northward where it junctioned with the Southern Pacific. The railroad company or the Army had evidently established a telegraph station at Imuris.

[20] Wood further elaborated on this incident in his personal narrative in Miles' memoirs (*Personal Recollections,* "Captain Leonard Wood's Story,") 506-517:

[The Peck family's] ranch was surrounded by the Indians, the entire family was captured, and several of the farm-hands were killed. The husband was tied up and compelled to witness indescribable tortures upon his wife until she died. The terrible ordeal rendered him temporarily insane, and as the Apaches . . . stand in awe of an insane person, they set him free; but otherwise he would never have been allowed to live. He was found afterwards by his friends wandering about the place.

The Lawton expedition later recovered the young Peck girl after the Apaches had carried her some three hundred miles. She was badly bruised but otherwise unharmed. See journal entry June 18.

[21] Chimney, an Apache, was Lawton's chief scout when the expedition began but because he feared being shot by Mexicans, he deserted. For days, Miles had been attempting to find him and persuade him to return. Miles to Lawton, May 10, 13, 1886. Lawton Papers.

[22] Dick was a veteran sergeant who served in several Apache campaigns. Thrapp, *Apachería*, 185.

[23] Charles A. P. Hatfield was a West Point graduate who served in the Department of Arizona from 1884 to 1888. He later commanded the 8th Cavalry in the Spanish-American War and the 5th Cavalry in the Philippine Insurrection. He retired as a colonel in 1914. George Cullum, *Biographical Register*, III, 195; V, 193.

[24] William Davis, or "Whispering Bill" as Wood later calls him, entered the Army as first lieutenant at the outset of the Civil War and received a regular army commission as Second Lieutenant in 1866. He rose to captain and retired in 1897. H. B. Heitman, *Historical Register and Dictionary of the United States Army* (Washington, 1903), 360.

[25] Robert A. Brown graduated from West Point in 1885 and served in the Department of Arizona until 1887. He later entered the Inspector General's Office and served as General Arthur McArthur's aide-de-camp in the Philippines, 1901-02. Promoted to brigadier general in the National Army in 1917, he participated in several battles in France, for which he was awarded the Croix de Guerre. He retired in 1923. Cullum, *Biographical Register*, III, 387; VIA, 369.

[26] Joseph H. Dorst graduated from West Point in 1873 and in 1886 was serving with the 4th Cavalry. He later served in the Philippines under General Franklin Bell. He retired in 1911. Frank Cook graduated from West Point in 1885, served with the 4th Cavalry, and resigned in 1886. *Ibid*, III, 210, 388; V, 201; VIA, 181.

[27] Wood never makes clear how it was decided who would walk or ride and when. The previous day both he and Benson walked while Lawton and Finley rode. Wood is quick to point out that he is able to walk while a regular officer, Finley, must ride.

[28] Literally, dried beef.

[29] Later, Wood found Johnson at Fort Huachuca under house arrest

Chasing Geronimo

awaiting trial or some other disposition. (Journal entry June 2). There is no record, however, that Johnson was ever courtmartialed.

[80] Calabasas (Spanish for pumpkin or gourd) was ten miles northwest of Nogales on the Sonora to Benson railroad. It was first settled in 1763 by the Jesuits. The town itself was started in 1865 by the Calabasas Land and Mining Company. It experienced a mining boom in the late 1860s but by 1886 it was in decline. Federal Writers' Project, Arizona, 302; Barnes, Arizona Place Names, 71; Frank Lockwood, Pioneer Days in Arizona (New York, 1938), 341-342.

[81] The conference concerned the intentions of the Indians who had returned to Arizona and appeared to be moving northward.

[82] John A. Dapray was Miles' aide-de-camp.

[83] Willcox (Wilcox) was on the Southern Pacific Railroad forty miles east of Benson. Named for General Orlando Willcox, commander of the Department of Arizona, 1880-82, it served as a shipping point and change station for Fort Grant, San Carlos Agency, Globe and other points north. Barnes, Arizona Place Names, 488; Bancroft, Arizona, 621. Miles described the town as "a miserable little collection of mud huts and small buildings . . . ," inhabited mostly by cowboys and saloonkeepers. Johnson, Unregimented General, 237.

[84] Pantano was a well-known early stage station and ranch. By 1886 the station had experienced many Apache raids and deprivations. One commentator wrote that the old cemetery near the station was filled with graves of men killed by the Apaches. Bancroft, Arizona, 316.

[85] Total Wreck Mining District was nine miles south of Pantano. The district received its name from the Total Wreck Mining Company, so called according to legend because the owner of the mine believed that to be the condition of the mineral formations in the mine. Barnes, Arizona Place Names, 450.

[86] Davidson's ranch was in Davidson canyon just south of Pantano. The Canyon, the spring near it, and hence the ranch probably received its name from a pioneer killed by the Apaches. Thrapp, Apachería, 115.

[87] This is an indication of how the "tough" frontier settler could vehemently complain to Washington about Indian depredations, but was quite willing to allow the Army to take all the chances in subduing them. Yet, the settlers were obviously not reluctant to risk their lives for a price.

[88] Old Baldy Mountain, also called Thomas' Peak, was one of the highest peaks (11,470 feet) in the White Mountains east of Fort Apache.

[89] Trailing Indians over this rugged terrain required great expertise. Those who did have the skill (usually limited to Indian scouts and a few white scouts) to follow the Apaches, however, could derive an incredible amount of information from a few clues. Frederic Remington graphically describes this:

Notes

> Here they [the Apaches] ran their horses, as is seen by the hoof-beats on the sand, and the droppings would indicate that the passage was made many hours before. That the Indians' horses were tired out can be seen by the jerky fall of feet, long strides shortening gradually, then long again as urged on by the cruel knife. They also passed in the night, for they have run into a mesquite bush instead of going around it. Then, too, they deemed themselves safe from immediate pursuit, as no scouts have lain back on the trail. All this and much more do the footmarks tell the experienced eyes that follow.

McCracken, *Remington's Own West*, 21.

[40] The ranch was named for the Tumacacori mission mentioned by Wood. The old mission, erected in the latter part of the sixteenth century, was on the Santa Cruz River about twelve miles northwest of Calabasas and ten miles from Nogales. The mission is still preserved and remains one of the great national monuments in the Southwest. Barnes, *Arizona Place Names*, 457; Federal Writer's Project, *Arizona*, 300; Earl Jackson, "Tumacacori's Yesterdays" *Southwest Monuments Association Popular Series*, no. 6, 1956.

[41] Tubac, meaning "adobe house," is the oldest town built by whites in Arizona. Established by the Spanish in 1752 as a presidio, it declined in importance when the presidio was moved four years later to Tucson. Isolated for one hundred years, mining operations in the 1850s revived it. Between 1858 and 1860, Arizona's first newspaper, the weekly *Arizonian*, was published in Tubac. Bancroft, *Arizona*, 381-83, 496-98; Barnes, *Arizona Place Names*, 453-454; William Bardsley, "Tubac, Little Town with a Big History," *Arizona Highways*, XXXIII (February, 1957), 36-39.

[42] William B. Royall was district commander at Fort Huachuca. Following a long service which included several battles in the Civil War and several Indian campaigns, Royall retired in 1887 because of "nervous irritability." Heitman, *Historical Register*, I, 849; National Archives, ACP Records, Record Group 94, File no. 4639. For a humorous example of Royall's "irritability" see James Parker, *The Old Army: Memories* (Phila., 1929), 135-136.

[43] Miss Agnes Royall was the colonel's daughter. Wood had been romancing Miss Royall since arriving at Fort Huachuca in September, 1885. Hermann Hagedorn, *Leonard Wood, a Biography* (New York, 1931), I, 64.

[44] See footnote 29, journal entry May 20.

[45] Fort Grant, twenty-five miles north of Willcox, was established in 1872. The original establishment on the Gila River was destroyed by a flood in 1866. Because of this and because of the unhealthy conditions of that location, it was moved to the base of Graham Mountain, a high snow-capped

Chasing Geronimo

peak north of Willcox. Barnes, *Arizona Place Names*, 184, 188. According
to Britton Davis, the new fort was built by forced Indian labor. Davis, *Geronimo*, 61. The military contingent was withdrawn in 1898 and the Fort
was abandoned; later it was turned over to the State of Arizona which set
up a reform school there. The old fort was also the site of the infamous Fort
Grant Massacre in 1871 when 146 civilians (Americans, Mexicans and Indians) fell upon a tribe of unsuspecting reservation Apache Indians, and in
full view of the fort killed more than one hundred men, women, and children. Thrapp, *Apachería*, 80-94; Thomas Farish, *History of Arizona* (Phoenix, 1918,) VI, 158-60; Frank Lockwood, *Apache Indians* (New York,
1938), 178.

⁴⁶ Charles Ward graduated from West Point in 1885. His was court
martialed and suspended from rank. He was reassigned to Fort Thomas,
Arizona, but was arrested for drunkenness again in September, 1887, court-
martialed a second time, and dismissed from service. Cullum, *Biographical
Register*, III, 181.

Drinking, a perennial pastime of all soldiers, was particularly common
among frontier soldiers because of the isolation and boredom of frontier
post life. More than a few officers like Lt. Ward became drinkers. Among
enlisted men alcoholism was especially high in the Army. Don Rickey records
that in the decade of the 1880s forty-one men for every one thousand hos-
pitalized were alcoholics. *Forty Miles a Day*, 159. See also pages 156-184
for a general discussion of drinking in the Indian-fighting Army.

⁴⁷ William A. Thompson entered the army as a private in 1862, rose to the
rank of first lieutenant during the war and was appointed second lieutenant
in 1866. He was a veteran of several Indian campaigns. When Miles arrived
in Arizona, he made Thompson his adjutant. Heitman, *Historical Register*,
I, 958.

⁴⁸ George Alexander Forsyth came up through the ranks from private in
1862 to major, USA, 1866. By 1886 he had made brigadier general, and was
already a famous Indian fighter. Ibid., 430. Virtually a legend in his own
day, he was described by young Remington as a soldier who carried "three
bullet wounds as mementos [of Indian campaigns] and all as lightly as a
buffalo would a charge of swan shot, and he is willing to absorb more lead
in the interest of the American Army." McCracken, *Remington's Own
West*, 25. After retiring Forsyth wrote a delightful account of his Army
career: *Thrilling Days in Army Life* (New York, 1900).

⁹⁴ That is, without the usual accoutrement. Actually, the campaign Army
operated under two kinds of marching orders: heavy and light. The former
usually meant approximately fifty pounds of campaign equipment, including
knapsack, half tent, extra shoes and clothes, rations for several days, and up
to 140 rounds of ammunition; for the cavalry all this plus horse equipment.

128

Notes

Light marching, or for the cavalry "stripped saddles," meant rations for only four days, one change of clothes and one hundred rounds of ammunition. Additional ammunition was carried on pack animals. Rickey, *Forty Miles a Day*, 221-225. For the best description of post-Civil War campaign equipment see James Hutchins, "The Cavalry Campaign Outfit at Little Big Horn," *Military Collector and Historian*, VII (Winter, 1956), 91-101.

[50] As "adjuncts" these Mexicans were probably intended as Scouts. Though there is no record of it, Miles probably sent them in a desperate effort to beef-up Lawton's forces. As Wood noted, they were of little use and the following day he managed somehow to get rid of them. They turn up again, however, near the end of the campaign. See journal entry for August 16.

CHAPTER 2

[1] The *aparejo* is a packsaddle still used extensively in Mexico. During the 1880s, it was very popular in southwestern United States. It was made of "two rectangular pads stuffed with a tough grass and joined by an unfilled section of leather which centers itself over an animal's backbone." Probably used in some form in the ancient world, it was brought to the New World by the Spanish. On top of the aparejo can be tied almost any object from a box to oil pipes. Although the Army had its own regulation packsaddle, the packers much preferred to use the aparejo. Sam Hicks, "Aparejo: the Perfect Packsaddle," *American West*, VI (January, 1969), 28-32.

[2] See Lawton to Miles, May 30, 1886. Lawton Papers.

[3] Zebina Nathaniel Streeter was a notorious renegade well-known throughout the Southwest. A rather enigmatic figure, his association with the Apaches was much more sinister than Wood indicates. He adopted Apache ways even to the point of fighting with them against whites. It was commonly believed that he visited white ranches and settlements, obtained information, and then led the Indians in raids against these same places. In 1883, he was declared an outlaw by the Arizona Territorial Legislature and a $5,000 reward was offered for his capture. Thrapp, *Apachería*, 279-280.

Miles, unfamiliar with his background, sent him to work for the Lawton expedition. He later warned Lawton that he had received information that Streeter was unreliable, but the old renegade remained with the expedition until the end. Miles to Lawton, May 9, 1886. Lawton Papers. Henry Flipper [see journal entry for July 3, footnote 8] also had an unfortunate experience with Streeter. See Theodore Harris, ed., *Negro Frontiersman: The Western Memoirs of Henry O. Flipper* (El Paso, 1963), 28.

[4] For a vivid description of the rugged terrain see Dudley Gordon, ed.,

129

Chasing Geronimo

"Lummis as a War Correspondent in Arizona," *American West*, II, (Summer, 1965), 4-12. Charles Lummis was a correspondent for the Los Angeles *Times* who campaigned with Crook for over a year.

[5] Wood was not the only one impressed by the incredibly profane vocabulary of the packers. Martha Summerhayes, newlywed wife of an Army officer, complained that the packer's oath "made my blood curdle. . . . The shivers ran up and down my back and I half expected to see [them] struck down by the hand of the almighty." When she remonstrated to her husband, he told her that " 'the mules wouldn't even stir to go up a hill, if they weren't swore at like that' ". Martha Summerhayes, *Vanished Arizona: Recollections of My Army Life* (M. M. Quaife, ed.) (Chicago, 1939), 80-82.

[6] Wood was very much impressed with Long but there is little information on his background. Farish cites a William Long as one of the discoverers of the productive Silver King Mine near Florence, Arizona. There is no evidence, however, that this the Billy Long of the Lawton expedition. Thomas Farish, *History of Arizona*, VI, 60.

[7] It was not unusual on an extended campaign for soldiers to wear out several pairs of shoes and ultimately turn to the Indian moccasin for footwear. Army shoes were manufactured at the military prison, Fort Leavenworth, Kansas. Made of notoriously bad leather, crudely constructed, some were sewn and others were fastened together by brass screws; but there was little difference between the two. In rugged country neither lasted more than a few days. The moccasin, which was tough, very comfortable, capable of withstanding water damage, was therefore much preferred by the soldiers to the Army issue shoe. Wood claimed in his official report that the men of the expedition paid as high as six dollars for Indian-made moccasins. For a discussion of Army clothing, including issue shoes, see Don Rickey Jr., *Forty Miles a Day*, 123-126.

[8] The United States had signed an agreement with Mexico in 1884 providing for the reciprocal crossing of the international border in pursuit of hostiles. See Headquarters, Department of Arizona, *General Orders*, no. 128, November 25, 1884. (Copy in Lawton Papers.)

[9] Tom Horn, interpreter of Spanish for many years under General Crook's Chief Scout, Al Sieber, was, after Sieber, the most prominent scout in the Southwest. Horn worked with Sieber at the San Carlos Agency, where he made friends with Geronimo and learned the Chiricahua Apache language. When Sieber became ill, Horn was sent with Crawford into Mexico and was with Crawford when the young Captain was shot. Lawton had been working without an experienced scout since the desertion of Chimney, and Miles persuaded Horn to join the Lawton expedition as chief scout.

Horn later served as packmaster for General William Shafter's command in Cuba in 1898 and took part in the Battle of San Juan Hill. After the Spanish-American War, he joined the Pinkerton Detective Agency. Accounts say that he candidly admitted his enjoyment of killing. In 1901, he was tried, convicted, and hanged for the murder of a fourteen year old boy.

For a personal account of Horn's life see his own *Life of Tom Horn, Government Scout and Interpreter, Written by Himself*, edited with an introduction by Dean Krakel (Norman, Okla., 1964). For a sketch of his life and work see Malone, *Dictionary of American Biography*, IX, 236. For his work with Crawford see Lt. Marion Maus' official report in Secretary of War, *Annual Report* (1886), 155-164, and also Maus' narrative in Nelson Miles, *Personal Recollections*, 450-479. For an unfavorable evaluation of Horn see Davis, *Geronimo*, 196. Two biographies have been written on Horn: Dean Krakel, *The Saga of Tom Horn* (Laramie, 1954), and Lauran Paine, *Tom Horn: Man of the West* (Barre, Mass., 1963), but there is still a need for a scholarly biography of this interesting man on the order of Dan Thrapp's work on Al Sieber.

CHAPTER 3

[1] Mescal, a favorite drink of the Mexicans, was a colorless alcoholic liquor made from the fermented juice of the agave plant. Britton Davis has a graphic description of the production of mescal and its effects, in *The Truth About Geronimo*, 155-56. The alcoholic content of mescal must have been extremely high. Although the Mexicans seemed able to consume great quantities without any ill effects, the Indians, less accustomed to this "firewater," invariably got roaring drunk on small amounts.

[2] Forgotten somewhere along the way was the idea that the Lawton expedition was to be composed of "picked men."

[3] Like most frontier Americans, including most soldiers, Wood held the Indian and rural Mexicans in contempt. Later in his life this racial prejudice became more pronounced. Some, like Lawton, despised the Mexicans more than the Indians.

[4] Jose Maria, a Mexican, was one of those shadowy characters, much like "Old Man" Streeter, who passed back and forth with equal facility between the white and Indian world. Farish accuses Jose Maria of organizing the Fort Grant Massacre. *History of Arizona*, III, 158-59. Frederic Remington, who met Jose Maria while visiting the San Carlos Agency, described him as a "villainous-looking Mexican" who, acting as interpreter for Miles, "shouts his interpretations at [the Indians] after the manner of a Mississippi River

mate in the boating days of old." McCracken, *Frederic Remington's Own West*, 20.

⁵ There is no indication, however, that this "fresh information" was worth very much or that it led them anywhere nearer the Indians. The trip was, in fact, unnecessary, the kind a cocky, self-assured young officer might make despite the opposition of a more experienced man. Even though Wood found evidence of some Indians near Sinoquipe, the expedition marched in the opposite direction on the following day.

⁶ An all too familiar Apache tactic.

⁷ Wood does not make very much of it in his journal, but wherever he went he dispensed medical aid to civilians. In the desolate area traversed by the expedition, where the Mexicans rarely if ever saw a doctor, "the lame, the halt, and the blind," as Lawton wrote his wife, flocked to Wood for treatment. Lawton was constantly struck by the incongruity of seeing Wood performing the duties of a tough young frontier officer one day and dispensing gentle medical help to the suffering of a desolate Mexican village on the next. Lawton to Mame, July 8, 1886. After a long hard ride, playing doctor to an entire town could be a burden. Once after a two-day ride, he had to perform several operations. "I did not appreciate being so well looked after," he wrote his mother. Wood to Mother, July 7, 1886, Wood Papers.

⁸ Henry Ossian Flipper was born a slave in 1856 in Thomasville, Georgia and reared in Atlanta. He entered West Point in 1873 and four years later became the first black man to graduate from the Military Academy. Upon graduation, he was assigned to the all-black 10th Cavalry, then on duty in the Southwest. In 1881, he was transferred to Fort Davis, Texas and assigned as commissary officer. The commander of the fort, Colonel William Shafter [see footnote 2, journal entry for May 4], accused Flipper of embezzlement of post funds and brought him to trial for this and for conduct unbecoming an officer. Flipper was aquitted of embezzlement but was convicted of the second charge and dismissed from the service on June 30, 1882. Flipper claimed at the time, and always believed, that his conviction was the result of Shafter's undisguised prejudice.

After dismissal, Flipper served for over thirty years as a civil and mining engineer on the mining frontier of Arizona and Mexico. Between 1893 and 1901, he served as a special agent for the Justice Department. In 1906, Albert B. Fall hired him as a consultant for his Sierra Mining Company. When Fall went to Washington in 1913 as senator, he appointed Flipper interpreter and translator for his sub-committee investigating American business interests in Mexico. Flipper also went with Fall into Department of Interior as assistant secretary, a position held from 1921 to 1923. When the Teapot Dome scandals broke, Flipper left the department and joined a petroleum company in Latin America. After eight years, he returned to Atlanta where he died in 1940. For a sketch of Flipper's life see the "Introduction" in Harris, *Negro Frontiersman*. The records of Flipper's court martial have been collected and microfilmed by the National Archives: "Records Relating to the Army Career of Henry Ossian Flipper, 1873-1883," (microcopy T-1027). Flipper himself has written two accounts of his life: the one previously cited and *The Colored Cadet at West Point, Autobiography of Lieutenant Henry O. Flipper* (New York, 1878).

According to Flipper, he was in the province of Chihuahua in 1886 "compiling maps for the Miner's Bank Company." He mentions in his memoirs camping with "his friend Captain Lawton," and talking extensively with a "civilian" doctor named Leonard Wood, whom he got to know "quite well." Harris, *Negro Frontiersman*, 27.

⁹ Strabismus is a disorder of vision, commonly called crosseye. An operation to correct strabismus was evidently not uncommon. Wood had received the best medical education offered in this country at that time. He had been a sound, if not brilliant, student at Harvard Medical School. Yet, he must have gained, at best, only a rudimentary knowledge of the strabismus disorder. He thus performed a delicate operation for which he had no particular skill or experience, and performed it under unsanitary conditions, knowing that he would be unable afterwards to give any further attention to the operation. He passed off the entire affair with the casual remark that it was "a rather good case for an operation."

¹⁰ Lawton had left the cavalry at Oposura for reasons given by Wood. Evidently they were sent back, because only the infantry went South with the expedition.

¹¹ The escape of the Indians, as Wood intimates, reduced the expedition's morale to a new low. Lawton was inclined to accept Crook's opinion that the Apaches could not be captured in twenty years. His exhausted cavalry had been left behind in Oposura; his infantry was down to fourteen available men after the July 14 encounter. Only Wood seemed to retain a faith in the expedition at this point. Lawton later acknowledged that Wood's unshakable confidence in the expedition, and "his untiring efforts to make it so," provided the spark that kept the command from disintegrating. "Lawton Report" in Report of the Secretary of War, *Annual Report* (1886), 180; Lawton to Mame, July 21, 1886. Lawton Papers.

CHAPTER 4

¹ Obviously only a small amount of medicine could be taken on an expedition such as this one. But in any sense, the Army did not provide the doctors

with a wide variety of medicines. Quinine, a bitter powder extracted from cinchona bark, was the common preventive and healing drug issued Army surgeons.

² Wood means the Arros or alternatively the Papigochic River, a small stream which empties into the Yaqui River near the village of Suaqui about six miles north of Sahuaripa.

³ That is, one of those Southerners who would not accept the outcome of the Civil War and chose exile, as did hundreds of ex-Confederates.

⁴ This ninety-mile trip is a fairly good indication not only of the frustration of the campaign but also of the desperate situation of the expedition at this point. Since Wood does not mention it, they apparently learned nothing of the whereabouts of the Indians. Thus, the expedition found itself deep in the wild, sparsely inhabited stretches of the Sierra Madre Mountains completely at a loss as to which way to turn. This condition continued for ten days more until Gatewood appeared with Miles' new policy.

⁵ A white powder used as a carthartic for worms.

⁶ The term *manta* usually designates the cheap cotton shawls or capes common in Latin America. But the horse blanket used to cover a pack animal's load was also called a manta. This is undoubtedly what Wood means.

⁷ The careers of Robert J. Walsh and Abiel L. Smith were very similar. Both were West Point graduates (Walsh, 1883, and Smith, 1887), both served in the 4th Cavalry in the Department of Arizona, both served also in the Philippines, and finally both achieved the rank of brigadier general. Smith retired in 1918 and Walsh in 1919. Cullum, *Biographical Dictionary*, III, 307, 373.

⁸ The daily thunderstorms that Wood described previously caused all the streams, including the Arros River, suddenly to flood.

CHAPTER 5

¹ While Lawton viewed the swollen river as just another depressing obstacle, it is evident that Wood saw it as a challenge, and crossing of it as something of a lark. It was another opportunity to prove his physical superiority. Parker comments in his memoirs that Wood was in "excellent spirits," while Lawton was in "as pessimistic mood." Parker, *The Old Army*, 177.

² James Parker graduated from West Point in 1876. He served on the frontier in Oklahoma, Texas, and Arizona, and later in Cuba and the Philippines, where he received the Medal of Honor for gallantry in action. In 1913 he was promoted to brigadier general and in 1919 to major general in the

National Army. He retired in 1918. He published one technical book (*Mounted Rifleman*, a manual on training cavalry) and an autobiography. Cullum, *Biographical Register*, III, 264; VIA, 215.

³ There is still some uncertainty as to Gatewood's position. Thrapp argues that Miles gave Gatewood an independent command, and thus Gatewood should be given credit for Geronimo's surrender. *The Conquest of Apachería*, 353-354. Thrapp claims Gatewood contacted Lawton because it was likely that only this expedition knew the whereabouts of Geronimo. There is no specific evidence for Wood's statement that Gatewood reported formally and in writing to Lawton. But there is no reason to doubt Wood's veracity, and Lawton certainly acted as though Gatewood were under his authority. Lawton to Mame, August 19, 26, 1886. Lawton Papers.

⁴ Gatewood's own account of his part in the campaign understandably makes no mention of his illness or his pessimism. Evidently Gatewood, a Crook man, was not enthusiastic about working with Miles or carrying out an assignment that would give all honors to Miles and his men, which was exactly the outcome. But in all fairness to Gatewood he was a very sick man who, for medical reasons, should never have been assigned so arduous a task. Charles B. Gatewood, "The Surrender of Geronimo," *Arizona Historical Review*, IV (April, 1931), 31. See Parker, *Old Army*, 175, and Lawton to Mame, August 26, 1886, Lawton Papers for Gatewood's pessimism. For a recent favorable view of Gatewood's work, see Thrapp, *Apachería*, 353-354. Thrapp believes that Parker's account must be taken with "a large measure of salt." However, Wood's journal and Lawton's letters support Parker's views.

⁵ To search for the Indians' trail.

⁶ "Bronco" was a term often used for Apaches, because like the small pony, they were considered wild and uncontainable.

⁷ Yet earlier Wood concluded that Gatewood, bothered by an inflamed bladder, found riding difficult. One has the impression that Wood would have sent back any other officer in Gatewood's condition. But the sickly Lieutenant was their last hope, and nothing short of total disability would have led Wood to give him a medical relief from duty.

⁸ W. B. Richardson graduated from West Point in 1884 and had been serving in the Department of Arizona since 1885. He was appointed brigadier general in the National Army in 1917 and served in France with the 39th Division. In March, 1919, he was assigned to command of the American troops in North Russia and later prepared for the General Staff a history of the Russian Expedition. Cullum, *Biographical Register*, III, 383.

Robert Lee Bullard graduated from West Point in 1885 and was assigned to the 10th Infantry. He later served in the Philippines and with the Provisional Government in Cuba after the intervention of 1906. In 1917 he was promoted to brigadier general and later to major general, the National Army, as commander of the Second Army in France. *Ibid.*, III, 390; V, 394.

[9] See journal entry for May 10, footnote 16.

[10] Britton Davis graduated from West Point in 1881. He, along with Crawford, became Crook's principal aide and foremost supporter. He was in command of the San Carlos Agency when the Chiricahua Apaches under Geronimo and Natchez escaped in 1885. Discouraged with the treatment of Crook, he resigned in 1886 and was appointed President of San Luis Mining Company in Pima Country, Arizona. Cullum, III, 353. For a controversial account of his work with the Indians and the Geronimo campaign see his *The Truth About Geronimo.*

[11] See journal entry for June 9, footnote 50.

[12] For interesting story on the inhabitants of Opoto (Oputo), see Davis, 165.

[13] Eugene Spencer graduated from West Point in 1882. Originally assigned to the 4th Cavalry, he transferred in 1884 to the Corps of Engineers and became the Engineer Officer for the Department of Arizona. Cullum, III, 357.

[14] General George Alexander Forsyth was a veteran of the Civil War and of several Indian campaigns. For a delightful account of his career see his *Thrilling Days in Army Life* (New York, 1900). [See footnote 48, Chapter 1]

[15] Wilbur Wilder graduated from West Point in 1877. He later served in the Philippines, the Punitive Expedition against Mexico in 1916 and in France in 1918. For courageous action in the Philippine Insurrection he received the Medal of Honor. Cullum, *Biographical Dictionary*, III, 280; VIA, 235. Wood uses the incorrect rank here; he later correctly identifies him as Lieutenant Wilder.

[16] Thomas Clay was the grandson of Henry Clay. After much pressure from political friends he was given a commission in 1877. He was retired for physical disability in 1894. National Archives. Record Group 94, ACP records.

[17] For once, at least, Wood is guilty of withholding information which serves to distort the facts. When one reads that Wood has "assumed authority" to give orders to Gatewood because "Lawton was busy," one immediately suspects Wood is not telling the whole story. A few sentences earlier Wood tells us that Lawton was furious at Gatewood's procrastination, and had "sent for [him] in post haste." What then occupied Lawton to such an extent that he was too busy to order Gatewood out personally? The fact is, Lawton was not busy; he was drunk.

The full story was later reconstructed by Thomas Clay and Robert Bullard. Wood, Clay, and Lawton went into Fronteras on August 22, as Wood reports. There they were given strong liquor by the prefect. Lawton drank heavily, and became exceedingly drunk, and began to abuse the Mexican soldiers. Wood and Clay managed to get him out of the saloon and into another room to allow him to sleep it off. Just at this point Gatewood arrived, according to Lawton's orders, and Wood assumed authority to speak for Lawton. Fearful that other officers were going to arrive in Fronteras and find Lawton drunk, Clay and Wood attempted to arouse Lawton in order to get him back to camp. As Clay later relates, Lawton jumped up and threatened him with a "heavy coffee cup." Clay, in turn, pulled his pistol on Lawton and threatened to shoot him. This sobered Lawton somewhat, and he immediately placed Clay under arrest. When they returned to camp, Wood interceded for Clay and persuaded Lawton to drop the charges. For Bullard's account see Bullard to Wood, February 13, 1901. Wood Papers. Clay's version may be found in the Hermann Hagedorn Papers. Hagedorn, who wrote the official biography of Wood, interviewed Clay extensively on the incident, but like Wood, he chose not to relate the entire story. Leonard Wood, a Biography (New York, 1931), II, 89.

CHAPTER 6

[1] Natchez (Nachite) was the son of Cochise. He was therefore the hereditary chief of the Chiricahua Apaches, but he was not their leader. Although noble in appearance and character, he apparently did not possess a dynamic enough personality to contain or lead such aggressive, older warriors as Geronimo.

[2] Skeleton Canyon was a famous rendezvous for Southwestern outlaws. Located at the southern end of the San Simon Mountains, it was called Cajon Bonito by the natives. Will C. Barnes, Arizona Place Names, 410; Britton Davis, The Truth About Geronimo, 79.

[3] A heliograph or heliostat was a device mounted on a tripod for signalling by means of a movable mirror which reflected beams of sunlight. Messages were sent in Morse Code (long or short flashes of light) by "alternately interposing and removing an object in front of the mirror." (Miles, Personal Recollections, 481-484.) Miles had used the instrument briefly in Montana and decided to put it to more extensive use in the Department of Arizona. Upon request, the Signal Corps sent Miles skilled officers and he placed them on high peaks throughout the Department. The system, once in full operation, was capable of sending messages over a distance of eight hundred miles in four hours. Between May and September, 1886, over two thousand messages were sent from fifty different stations. Miles was much impressed with the system, believing that it was instrumental in the capture of Geron-

imo. For a detailed, technical description of the use of the heliograph see U.S. Army, Department of Arizona, *Reoprt of General Practice of the Heliograph System in Arizona* (Washington, 1890).

⁴ James B. Richards (West Point, 1878), later conducted the Indians to Fort Marion, Florida. Cullum, *Biographical Register*, III, 304.

⁵ Located on the Arizona-Mexico border.

⁶ Meaning that Smith held his commission longer than Gatewood and could technically claim to be his superior officer.

⁷ The Smith incident was of only minor importance. The Indians were excited by Miles' reluctance to meet with them, which prolonged the final surrender and made them vulnerable to an attack by the Mexicans.

⁸ Morris Foote entered the Army as a private in 1862. He ultimately rose to a brigadier geenral in 1903. Heitman, *Historical Register*, 427.

⁹ Roger Ames was a Negro officer in the 10th Cavalry. Wood's later claim that Ames was "anxious to get in among white troops" may tell a great deal more about Wood than Ames.

¹⁰ The controversy over the disposition of Geronimo's band is discusssed in detail in the epilogue.

EPILOGUE

¹ Sheridan to Miles, August 24, 1886. National Archives. Adjutant General's Office, Record Group 94, File No. 2025. Hereafter cited as N.A., RG 94.

² Lawton to Mame, September 2, 1886. Lawton Papers, Library of Congress.

³ See Wood's journal entry for September 8.

⁴ Sheridan to Miles, September 7, 1886; Drum to Miles, September 8, 1886. N.A., RG 94.

⁵ O. O. Howard to Drum, September 17, 1886. N.A., RG 94.

⁶ Drum to Howard, September 18, 1886, *Ibid*.

⁷ Miles to Drum, September 29, 1886, *Ibid*.

⁸ Martin Schmitt, *General Crook, His Autobiography.* (Norman, Oklahoma), 263.

⁹ *Ibid.*, 264.

¹⁰ Hermann Hagedorn, *Leonard Wood, A Biography*, I (New York, 1931), 104.

¹¹ Stanley to Drum, September 30, 1886. Actually, Geronimo and his band did not immediately join their families imprisoned at Fort Marion, St. Augustine. Instead, they were transferred to old Fort Pickens near Pensacola; not

Notes

until April, 1887, did their families join them at Fort Pickens. One year later the entire group was sent to Mount Vernon, Alabama. General Crook, who along with friends in Congress continued to work for better treatment of the Chiricahuas, finally succeeded in getting the Indians transferred to Fort Sill, Indian Territory, where the climate was better for them than in Alabama. Schmitt, General Crook, 290-300.

[12] Report of Captain Henry Lawton in Secretary of War, Annual Report, 1886. Ten years later, when Wood was being considered for the Medal of Honor, Lawton further elaborated on Wood's service:

> ". . . he uncomplainingly endured personal inconvenience [so] that his example might encourage those under his charge . . ."
> Lawton to Miles, May 13, 1894. Copy in Wood Papers, Library of Congress.

[13] Copy in Wood Papers. Both Lawton and Miles had received Medals of Honor during the Civil War.

[14] In 1887, Miles succeeded General O. O. Howard as commander of the Division of the Pacific; in 1894, after being promoted to major general, he was assigned as commander of the Department of the East. One year later he began his stormy career as commanding general of the Army. Virginia Johnson, The Unregimented General: A Biography of Nelson A. Miles (Boston, 1962); Edward Ransom, "Nelson A. Miles as Commanding General, 1895-1903," Military Affairs, XXIX (Winter, 1965-66), 179-200.

Within two years after the Geronimo campaign Lawton had been promoted to colonel. During the Spanish-American War he served in Cuba as major general in command of a volunteer brigade, and after the war briefly as military governor of Santiago Province. He was later assigned as commander of a brigade in the Philippines where he was killed in action on December 19, 1899. Dumas Malone, ed., Dictionary of American Biography, XI (New York, 1933), 62-63; O. O. Howard, "Lawton's Long Service," Review of Reviews, XXI (February, 1900), 184-186.

Despite his concern during the Geronimo campaign, Lawton later complained to Wood that Miles was no great help in getting advancements. Lawton to Wood, January 11, 1888. Wood Papers.

[15] Gatewood, "Surrender of Geronimo," 31.

[16] Parker, Old Army, 189.

Selected Bibliography

PRIMARY SOURCES

Manuscripts

Papers of Hermann Hagedorn, Library of Congress.
Papers of Leonard Wood, Library of Congress.
Papers of Henry Lawton, Library of Congress.

Unpublished Documents

National Archives, Records of the Adjutant General's Office, (Record Group 94).
"Records Relating to the Army Career of Henry O. Flipper, 1873-1883" (Microcopy T-1027). (Collected from Record Group 94 and 153.)

Published Documents

House Executive Documents. Report of the Secretary of War. Annual Report, Vol. 1. 2nd Session, 49th Cong., 1886. Washington: GPO, 1886.
Senate Documents. "The Capture of Geronimo," no. 117. 2nd Sess., 45th Cong., 1886. Washington: GPO, 1886.
U.S. Army, Department of Arizona, Report of General Practice of the Heliograph in Arizona. Washington: Army Signal Office, 1890.

PERSONAL ACCOUNTS

Books

Betzinez, Jason. I Fought With Geronimo. Harrisburg, Pa.: The Stackpole Company, 1959.
Bigelow, John. On the Bloody Trail of Geronimo. Edited by Arthur Woodward. Los Angeles: Westernlore Press, 1958.
Bourke, John G. An Apache Campaign in the Sierra Madre. New York: Charles Scribner and Sons, Second Edition, 1958.
Bourke, John. On the Border With Crook. New York: Scribner's Sons, 1891.
Davis, Britton. The Truth About Geronimo. New Haven: Yale University Press, Second Printing, 1963.
Forsyth, George A. Thrilling Days in Army Life. New York: Harper and Brothers, 1900.

Harris, Theodore, ed. *Negro Frontiersman: The Western Memoirs of Henry Ossian Flipper, First Negro Graduate of West Point.* El Paso: Western College Press, 1963.

Horn, Tom. *Life of Tom Horn, Government Scout and Interpreter, Written By Himself.* Norman, Okla., 1964.

McCracken, Harold, ed. *Frederic Remington's Own West.* New York: Dial Press, 1961.

Miles, Nelson A. *Personal Recollections and Observations of General Nelson A. Miles.* Chicago: The Werner Company, 1896.

Miles, Nelson A. *Serving the Republic: Memoirs of the Civil and Military Life of Nelson A. Miles.* New York: Harper and Brothers, 1911.

Parker, James. *The Old Army: Memories, 1872-1918.* Phila.: Dorrance and Company, 1929.

Schmitt, Martin, ed. *General George Crook, His Autobiography.* Norman, Okla.: University of Oklahoma Press, 1960.

Sheridan, Philip H. *Personal Memoirs of Philip H. Sheridan.* 2 Vols. New York: Appleton Company, 1902.

Summerhayes, Martha. *Vanished Arizona: Recollections of My Army Life* (M. M. Quaife, ed.). Chicago: Lakeside Press, 1939.

Articles

Daly, H. W. "The Geronimo Campaign." *Arizona Historical Review,* III (July, 1930).

Clay, Thomas. "Some Unwritten Incidents of the Geronimo Campaign." *Proceedings of the Annual Meeting, Order of Indian Wars* (Jan. 26, 1929).

Clum, John P. "Geronimo." *New Mexico Historical Review,* III (October, 1928).

Crook, George. "The Apache Problem." *Journal of Military Service Institute of the United States,* VII (October, 1886).

Gatewood, Charles B. "The Surrender of Geronimo." *Arizona Historical Review,* IV (April, 1931).

Gordon, Dudley, ed. "Lummis as a War Correspondent in Arizona." *American West,* II (Summer, 1965).

SECONDARY SOURCES

Books

Arizona Department of Mineral Resources. *Mining in Arizona: Its Past, Its Present, Its Future.* Phoenix: 1953.

Bancroft, Hubert H. *History of Arizona and New Mexico, 1530-1888.* San Francisco: The History Company, 1889.

Bibliography

Barnes, Will C. *Arizona Place Names*. University of Arizona Bulletin, Vol. II, no. 1. Tucson, 1935.

Brandes, Ray. *Frontier Military Posts of Arizona*. Globe, Ariz.: D.S. King, 1960.

Caesar, Gene. *Rifle For Rent, a Dramatic True Story of the Most Colorful Figures of the Untamed Southwest*. Derby, Conn.: Monarch Books, 1963.

Clum, Woodworth. *Apache Agent, the Story of John P. Clum*. New York: Houghton Mifflin, 1936.

Cullum, George. *Biographical Register of the Officers and Graduates of the Military Academy*. Boston: Houghton Mifflin, 1891-1923.

Downey, Fairfax. *Indian-Fighting Army*. New York: Charles Scribner's Sons, 1941.

Federal Writer's Project. *Arizona: A State Guide*. New York: Hastings House, 1940.

Farish, Thomas. *History of Arizona*. 8 Vols. Phoenix: Filmer Brothers, 1918.

Ganoe, William. *The History of the United States Army*. New York: Appleton Company, 1942.

Hagedorn, Hermann. *Leonard Wood, A Biography*. New York: Harper and Brothers, 1931.

Heitman, H. B. *Historical Register and Dictionary of the United States Army*. 2 Vols. Washington: GPO, 1903.

Johnson, Virginia. *The Unregimented General: A Biography of Nelson A. Miles*. Boston: Houghton Mifflin, 1962.

Krakel, Dean. *The Saga of Tom Horn*. Laramie: Powder River Publications, 1954.

Leckie, William. *The Buffalo Soldiers*. Norman: University of Oklahoma Press, 1967.

Lockwood, Francis. *The Apache Indians*. New York: The Macmillan Company, 1938.

Lockwood, Francis. *Pioneer Days in Arizona*. New York: The Macmillan Company, 1940.

Malone, Dumas, ed. *Dictionary of American Biography*. 20 Vols. New York: Charles Scribner's Sons, 1928-1936.

Mazzonovich, Anton. *Trailing Geronimo*. Los Angeles: Gem Publishing Company, 1926.

Procter, Gil. *Tucson, Tubac, Tumacacori*. Tucson: Arizona Silhouettes, 1956.

Ogle, Ralph. *Federal Control of Western Apaches, 1848-1886*. Albuquerque: New Mexico Historical Society Publications, 1940.

Paine, Lauran. *Tom Horn, Man of the West*. Barre, Mass.: Barre Publishing Company, 1963.

Chasing Geronimo

Public Library of Fort Wayne, Indiana. *Major General Henry W. Lawton of Fort Wayne, Indiana.* 1954.

Rickey, Don, Jr. *Forty Miles A Day on Beans and Hay: The Enlisted Soldier Fighting the Indians Wars.* Norman: University of Oklahoma Press, 1963.

Spaulding, Oliver. *The United States Army in War and Peace.* New York: Putnam Company, 1937.

Thrapp, Dan. *Al Sieber: Chief of Scouts.* Norman: University of Oklahoma Press, 1964.

Thrapp, Dan. *The Conquest of Apachería.* Norman: University of Oklahoma Press, 1967.

Utley, Robert. *Frontiersmen in Blue, 1848-1865.* New York: The Macmillan Company, 1967.

Weigley, Russell. *History of the United States Army.* New York, The Macmillan Company, 1967.

Articles

Balestrero, Phyllis. "Nogales." *Arizona Highways,* XXXIV (September, 1958).

Bandelier, A. F. "Removal of Apaches from Arizona." *Nation,* XLIII (1886).

Bardsley, William. "Tubac, Little Town With A Big History." *Arizona Highways,* XXXIII (February, 1957).

Bloom, Lansing B. "Bourke on the Southwest." *New Mexico Historical Review,* X (January, 1935).

Coffman, Edward. "Army Life on the Frontier, 1865-1898." *Military Affairs,* XX (Winter, 1956).

Gaines, William H. "Boldly and Alone." *Virginia Cavalcade,* V (Spring, 1956)

Greever, William S. "Railway Development in the Southwest." *New Mexico Historical Review,* XXXII (April, 1957).

Hutchins, James. "The Cavalry Campaign Outfit at Little Big Horn." *Military Collector and Historian,* VII (Winter, 1956).

Jackson, Earl. "Tumacacori's Yesterdays." *Southwest Monuments Association Popular Series,* 6 (1956).

Nalty, Bernard and R. S. Strobridge. "Captain Emmet Crawford, Commander of Apache Scouts." *Arizona and the West,* IX (Spring, 1964).

Ransom, Edward. "Nelson A. Miles as Commanding General, 1895-1903." *Military Affairs,* XXIX (Winter, 1965-66).

Bibliography

Sims, Harper. "The Incredible Story of the Chiricahua Scouts." *Western Brand Book*, XIII (August, 1956).

Stover, William. "The Last of Geronimo and His Band." *Frontier Times*, (January, 1953).

Taylor, Fenton. "So They Built Fort Bowie." *Desert Magazine*, XIV (August, 1951).

Index

Agua Caliente, 42

Agua Seca, 37

Alias, Jose Maria: joins expedition, 62; fights with Scouts, 96; hostiles from Geronimo's band talk with wife of, 98, 100; shadowy character, 131; Frederic Remington comments on, 131-132

Alias Creek, 107-108

Allsup: joins expedition, 51; of no use to expedition, 52, 56; out shooting with Wood, 54

Ames, Roger: joins expedition, 109; disturbs hostiles, 111; Wood comments on, 111, 138

Andrews, George, 35

Apache Indians: perfect guerrilla warfare, 6, 20; characteristics, 6; and Crook, 6-8; acclimated to desert conditions, 9-10; noted, 117

Apache Scouts: key Crook policy, 7, 8; Sheridan lost confidence in, 9; work with the expedition, 13, 14, 15, 17, 26, 27, 30, 31, 34, 41, 43, 54, 56, 62, 63, 66, 71-72, 73, 75, 81, 83, 88, 90, 91, 95, 96, 100, 101

Aparejo: expedition packers use as packsaddle, 50; history, 129

Arispe, Mexico, 19

Arizona House, Wood eats dinner at, 44

Army: description of post-war Indian fighting, 4-6; and the Apaches, 6, 20

Arros River: 15, 16, 20, 75, 82, 83, 91; description, 134; flood, 134

Banamachi, 60

Bannister, Doctor, 93, 97, 109

Babocomari River, 27

Barrows, Charles, 39

Benson, Henry C.: joins expedition as supply officer, 29; work as supply officer, 34, 35, 37, 39, 45, 46, 49, 59, 68, 95; Lawton complains of immaturity of, 124

Benson Junction, 44

Benadine Ranch, 108

Bourke, John G., memoirs cited, 21

Brown, Dr. Paul, 27, 44

Brown, Robert A.: joins expedition, replacing Finley as officer in command of the Scouts, 35; work as commander of Scouts, 61, 62, 63, 66, 68, 69, 81, 83, 100, 101; flanking march with Scouts on Geronimo's camp, 71-72; Wood doctored by, 74; Lawton aided by, 75; tries to contain drunken scouts, 96

Index

Brown, William, 26
Bullard, Lt. Robert L.: noted, 93, 97, 109, 119; career sketched, 135; account of Clay's fight with Lawton, 136-137

Calabasas: 14, 15, 38, 39, 43, 44, 45, 50; history, 126
Calomel: 79; description, 134
Cave Creek, 110
Chicken, Indian Scout, 88
Chimney, Scout: 34; Lawton's chief scout, 125; his desertion, 125
Chiricahua Mountains, 110
Clarke, Powhattan: bravery in Lebo battle, 28, 124; career sketched, 124
Clay, Thomas: joins expedition, 99; noted, 101, 106, 107: career sketched, 136; fight with Lawton, 136-137
Cleveland, President Grover: uncertain about disposition of hostiles, 113; orders hostiles sent to nearest fort, 114, 115; directs department commander at San Antonio to confer with Geronimo, 116
Columbia Smelter, 42
Cook, Frank: 35; career sketched, 125
Crawford, Emmet: and Apache Scouts, 8, 119; death in Mexico noted, 18, 25, 105; description, 121
Crittendon: 27, 44; history, 123
Crook, George: assigned as commander of Dept. of Arizona, 6; noted 9, 10, 20, 25; career and policy evaluated, 6-7; resigns as commander, 8, 26, 121; apologia cited, 21; engaging personality, 122; Miles criticized by, 122

Cumpas (Mexico), 62, 64, 104

Daly, H. L.: 26; well-known packer, 122; with Crawford expedition, 122; inaccurate article on Lawton expedition, 122
Dapray, John A.: 38, 44, 45, 109; Miles' aide-de-camp, 126
Davidson's Ranch: 40; history, 126
Davis, Britton: Crook's trusted aide, 7; book on Geronimo campaign cited, 21; noted, 95; career sketched, 136
Davis, William: reports Indian trail to expedition, 34; noted, 39, 40, 41; career sketched, 125
Davis, Wirt, 25
Dick, Scout: 34, 55; veteran first sergeant of Scouts, 125
Dorst, Joseph H.: 35; career sketched, 125
Drum, Hugh A. (Adjutant General): instructions to Miles on disposition of Apaches, 114; dispute with Miles over disposition, 115

Edwaddy, 82, 90, 93, 104
Elgin Station: 27; history 123

Finley, Leighton: placed in charge of Apache Scouts, 26; R. A. Brown replaces, 60; work with Scouts, 33, 34, 37, 38, 45, 57, 58; noted, 29, 32, 35, 36
Flipper, Henry O.: camped near expedition, 64, 65; life and career sketched, 132-133; court-martialed while serving under William Shafter, 132
Foote, Morris: 109; career sketched, 138

Index

Forsyth, George A.: 45, 99; career sketched, 128, 136; described by Remington, 128; memoir cited, 136

Fort Bowie: Apaches dispatched from, 19, 110, 113, 114; noted, 111, 116; history, 122

Fort Grant: Wood witness before court-martial at, 44; history, 127; massacre at, 128

Fort Huachuca: Wood arrives at, 5, 12; Miles arrives at and establishes headquarters at, 11, 122; noted, 13, 15, 42, 44, 45, 46, 49, 50, 51, 52, 56, 59, 60, 93; history, 122

Fort Marion, Florida, Apaches dispatched to, 19, 113, 115

Fort Pickens, Florida, Geronimo and band transferred to, 138

Fort Sill, Indian Territory, final home of Geronimo, 139

Fronteras: Indians reported near, 98; expedition moves near, 100; contact made with hostiles at, 100; noted, 98, 99, 101, 104, 105, 136, 137

Frost, Hank, in charge of Nogales "Scouts," 46

Frisbee, Jack, 61

Gatewood, Charles: joins expedition with new policy from Miles, 17, 88; lacks confidence in his mission, 18, 88, 92; meets with Geronimo, 18, 101; formally reports to Lawton, 88; ordered by Lawton into Fronteras, 98; Lawton annoyed at dilatoriness of, 98-99; ordered out by Wood, 100; moving northward with hostiles, 106; friction with A. L. Smith, 108; noted as a Crook man, 117; obscure career after campaign, 118; believed responsible for capture of hostiles, 118

Geronimo: leader of hostiles, 4, 8, 25, 103; and Crook, 8, 26; Miles' strategy for capture of, 9-11, 17; Gatewood parleys with, 18, 104; disposition of, 20, 112, 113-114, 117; describes chase, 104; visits Lawton's camp, 104, 106; prepared to fight Mexicans, 106; Miles parleys with, 109-110, 113; leaves Fort Bowie, 111-112; noted, 13, 15, 18, 19, 20, 21, 87, 103

Gilaville, 110

Guadalupe Canyon: 108; location, 138

Guaymas, 77

Hatfield, C.A.P.: 34, 35; career sketched, 125

Heliograph: 108; description, 137; Miles' use of, 137-138

Hermosillo, 32

Horn, Tom: joins expedition as chief Scout, 57; swims flooded river, 83; scouting work, 88, 92; shot at by hostiles, 94; involved in fight with drunken scouts, 96; noted, 97, 99, 105; life and scouting career sketched, 130-131; need for scholarly biography, 131

Huepari, 97

Imuris, Mexico, 31, 32, 34

Johnson, Carter, 39, 40, 41

Johnson, Henry: in charge of infantry, 13, 26, 27, 29; relieved from duty for drinking, 37, 39; under house arrest at Fort Huachuca, 44, 125-126

Index

Kimball, A. S., 45

La Punca, 98

Las Pinas Mountains, 29

Lawton, Henry W.: background, 10-11; appointed commanding officer of the expedition, 10, 26; and Miles, 14, 16, 32, 38-39, 40, 49, 103, 139; and Gatewood, 17, 88, 100, 135; and Mexican irregulars, 18-19, 55-56, 105-106, 108-109; leads attack on hostiles' camp, 70-72; eats spoiled corn beef, 94-95; trouble at Fronteras, 99-100; and Geronimo, 104; praises Wood, 116-117; and Clay, 136-137; career after 1886, 139

Lebo, T. C.: battle with hostiles praised, 28, 123; career sketched, 123; noted, 38, 39

Long, Billy: civilian courier for expedition, 38; work as courier, 46, 52, 95, 101; trailing with Horn, 57

Lummis, Charles, correspondent with Crook, 130

McCullough's Ranch, 28

Magdalena River, 31

Malpais Ranch, 34

Maus, Marion: noted, 108; Crawford's aide, 121

Mescal, 59, 131

Mescal Ranch, 58

Mescatel Ranch, 28

Mexican irregulars: destroy hostiles' trail, 15; and the expedition, 55-56; 105-106, 108-109; concealed in Fronteras, 100; kill Crawford, 121

Miles, Nelson A.: background, 8-9; appointed commander of Department, 9, 26; campaign strategy, 9-10, 13, 17, 38-39, 134; and Crook, 9, 10, 26, 122; memoirs cited, 21; and Lawton, 14, 16, 38-39, 49, 103, 117-118; and Gatewood, 17, 18, 118; and Geronimo, 18, 19; controversy over disposition of Geronimo, 20-21, 104, 109, 110, 112, 113-116, 138; and Wood, 26, 44, 45, 112, 117-118; praises Wood, 116; and heliograph, 137-138; career after 1886 sketched, 139

Montoya: joins expedition, 33; noted, 36

Nacori, 26, 78, 80

Nacori Creek, 17, 79, 82, 89, 94, 95

Nacori-Sahuaripa Trail, 75, 79, 87

Natchez: outbreak led by, 25, 26; hereditary chief, 104, 137; out looking for brother, 109; escape by brother of, 111; life sketched, 137

Nogales: 28, 37, 46, 22; history, 123

Nogales "Scouts": Benson refuses to supply, 46; in charge of Hank Frost, 46; accompanying, James Parker's company, 97

Ojo de Agua, 34, 46, 50

Old Baldy Mountain: 42; history, 126

Oposura: 64, 65, 68, 81; Lawton leaves cavalry in, 133

Opoto, 34, 97

Pantano; 39, 40, 41, 50; history, 126

Parker, James: escorts Gatewood to expedition, 17, 88; memoirs cited, 21; started north from expedition,

Index

92; with Nogales "Scouts," 97; comments on Lawton's response to Gatewood mission cited, 120

Patch, Alexander, 45

Peck family: Wood describes hostile capture of, 32, 125; daughter recovered from hostiles by expedition, 55, 56, 125

Pickett, Dr. William M., Confederate exile, 77

Pinto Mountains, 98

Ranches, general description, 122-123; see individual names

Remington, Frederic: discusses Lebo battle, 124; describes methods of trailing Indians, 126-127

Richards, James B.: 108, 109; transported Apaches to Florida, 138

Richardson, W. B.: 93, 98, 104; career sketched, 135

Rincon, 32, 35

Rincon Ranch, 29

Royall, Agnes: 44; Wood romances, 127

Royall, William B.: 44, 45, 51; career sketched, 127

Sahuaripa, 74, 76, 78, 93

San Bernardino, 103, 104, 107, 108

San Carlos Reservation, 8, 33, 61, 119

San Lazaro, 35

Santa Barbara Ranch, 50

Santa Cruz River, 28, 38, 42

Santa Teresa Mining District, 53

Scott, Corporal: leg amputated, 28; Powhattan Clarke saves life, 124

Shafter, William: 26, 44; career sketched, 121-122

Sheridan, Philip: commanding general of the Army, 17; lost confidence in Crook, 17; instructs Miles to hold hostiles at Fort Bowie, 114

Sherman, John, 9

Sherman, William, 9

Sinoquipe, 57, 58, 60, 62, 63

Skeleton Canyon: site of Geronimo's surrender, 19, 104; note, 109, 116; history, 137

Smith, Abiel L.: works with Wood in crossing flooded river, 87; approaches Mexican irregulars, 105; friction with Gatewood, 108; career sketched, 134; antagonizes hostiles, 138-139

Sonora Land Company, 35-36

Sonora Province, Mexico, 13, 15, 29, 45, 106

Sonoro River, 57

Southern Pacific Railroad, 39, 123

Spencer, Lieutenant: 98; career sketched, 136

Strabismus: 65; description of, 133; Wood performs delicate operation without real experience, 133

Streeter, Zebina N.: joins expedition, 51; called White Apache, 51; raises false alarm, 52, 53; noted, 57, 58, 64; notorious career described, 128; experience with Henry Flipper noted, 129

Summerhayes, Martha: comments on ranches noted, 127; comments on packer's profanity noted, 130

Taracahi Ranch, 99

Tepachi, 65, 67

Tepachi Ranch, 89

Territt, Lieutenant: joins expedition in command of infantry, 39; noted, 41, 43; relieved by Lawton, 50, 51

Index

Tevis, James H., memoirs noted, 123

Tevis Ranch: 27; history, 123

Thompson, William A.: 44, 46, 112, 114; career sketched, 128; Miles' adjutant, 128

Tony (Scout): assigned first sergeant of Scouts, 61; noted 68, 96

Total Wreck Mining District: 40; history, 126

Tubac: 43; history, 127

Tucson, 37, 39, 41, 42, 45

Tumacacori Mission: 43, history, 127

Ures, 90, 93

Virginia Hotel, 45

Walsh, Robert: joins expedition as officer in command of the infantry, 37; left in Calabasas, 43; with a grievance, 95; disturbed because horses missing, 102; with Gatewood and hostiles, 106; career sketched, 134

Ward, Charles: 44; career sketched, 128

Wilder, Wilbur: camped near Fronteras, 99; talked with hostiles' women in Fronteras, 100; with Miles, 109; career sketched, 136

Willcox: 38, 44; history, 126

Wilson, Jack, 56, 82, 93, 104

Wood, Leonard: background, 3-4; 11-12; on expedition in 1885, 12; views on Miles, 13; appointed to Lawton expedition, 13; bitten by a spider, 16, 69, 74, 75; estimate of Crook, 21, 121, 122; describes Mexican settlements, 36, 37, 67, 76-77, 89; purchases food for expedition, 38, 49; exhausting trip to Vantano, 41-43, 117; transports supplies, 45-46, 49-54; officer of insubordinate infantry, 60, 64; work with Scouts, 61, 62, 89-92; medical work on expedition, 64, 65, 94-95, 132, 133; on Army equipment, 66, 81, 130; description of attack on hostiles' camp, 70-72; on expedition's food, 79, 82, 93, 95, 100, 124; views on Gatewood, 88, 98, 99, 135, 136; struggle with drunken scouts, 96; ordered Gatewood out, 100, 135, 136; and Mexican irregulars, 104-107; in Geronimo's camp, 107; and Natchez, 108, 110; commended by Miles and Lawton, 116-117; awarded Medal of Honor, 117, 118; identifies ranches, 122-123; views on packers, 52, 130

Wratten, George, interpreter for Gatewood, 98, 107

Yaqui River, 16, 70, 79, 93